IN MALAYSIA

IN MALAYSIA

**Stella Martin
and
Denis Walls**

BRADT PUBLICATIONS

First published 1986 by Bradt Publications, 41 Nortoft Road, Chalfont St Peter, Bucks SL9 0LA, UK

Copyright © 1986 Stella Martin and Denis Walls

All rights reserved. No part of this publication may be reproduced, stored in a retrieval system or transmitted in any form or by any means, electronic, mechanical, photocopying, recording, or otherwise, without the prior written permission of the copyright holders.

British Library Cataloguing in Publication Data

Walls, Denis
   In Malaysia.
   1. Malaysia—Description and travel
   I. Title   II. Martin, Stella
   915.95′0453   DS592.6

   ISBN 0-946983-03-8

Photographs by the authors
Front cover: A Chinese opera star relaxing backstage
Back cover: A Thaipusam devotee

Illustrations by Brenda Katté
Designed and typeset by Allset Composition, London
Printed and bound in Great Britain by
A. Wheaton and Company Ltd, Exeter, Devon

To the children of our Malay neighbours who looked after Liam and gave us time to write this book

Pangkor Island.

Contents

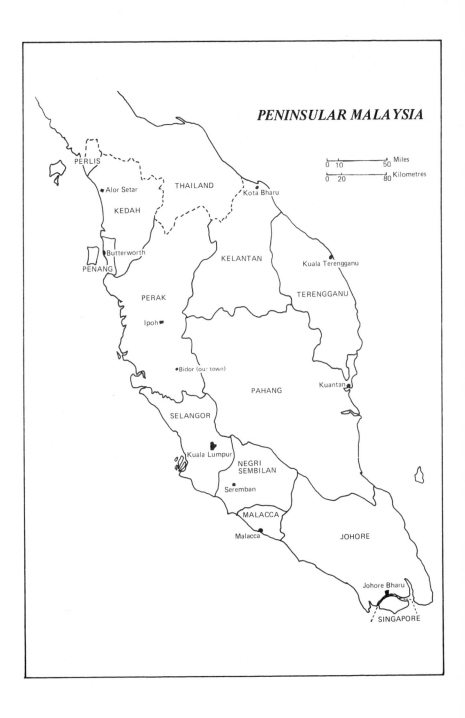

PENINSULAR MALAYSIA

Miles
0 10   50
0   20   80 Kilometres

PERLIS

• Alor Setar   THAILAND

KEDAH   Kota Bharu

• Butterworth   KELANTAN   Kuala Terengganu •

PENANG

PERAK   TERENGGANU

Ipoh •

• Bidor (our town)   Kuantan •

PAHANG

SELANGOR

Kuala Lumpur

NEGRI
SEMBILAN

• Seremban

MALACCA

Malacca •   JOHORE

Johore Bharu

SINGAPORE

Preface

In a country as racially mixed as Malaysia, the English language during colonial times was quite naturally adopted as the lingua franca among the predominantly Chinese and Indian urban population. It was also natural that after independence the new Malay-dominated government should want to replace English with Malay as the common language of all Malaysians.

It took independent Malaysia more than 20 years to phase out English completely as a medium of instruction in state schools but it was not long afterwards that the government became worried about the dramatically falling standard of English and the adverse long-term effects it might have on the country. For business purposes and overseas study a working knowledge of English is essential. It was the government decision to arrest the decline of English which led to us being in Malaysia.

More than 200 English teachers were recruited on three-year contracts from Britain and Australia over a period of five years (1979—84) and sent to teach mainly in the more educationally-deprived rural and semi-rural areas of Malaysia. For many of us it was an uphill battle but our efforts were rewarded with small increases in the all-important third year exam pass rates.

The three and a half years spent in Malaysia, however, had greater personal significance for the two of us. During our time there we not only learnt a great deal about a variety of very different cultures but we also met, married and had our son Liam. When our contracts ended we found ourselves reluctant to leave a country which had come to mean so much to us without making some sort of written record of our experiences there. What we have produced is both a personal account of our stay and a comprehensive description of the country, its people and their beliefs. A factual guide to out-of-the-way places, many of which are not mentioned in more conventional guides, completes the book and should prove useful to residents and visitors who are interested in taking more than a superficial glance at Malaysia.

1

Approaches

Most of the book was written by us jointly and as a result our individuality tends to disappear into an amorphous 'we'; hence this chapter – our separate (and, we hope, not too sentimental) accounts of our independent arrivals in Malaysia and our meeting there which was the beginning of the whole story.

Stella

Snow flurried past the window of the train which had been standing stationary in the same patch of forest for the past hour. Altogether we had covered no more than ten miles that day.

"This is a very good train for tourists," said the lugubrious Dane who shared my cabin. "It stops often for them to admire the Soviet countryside."

We had been on the trans-Siberian express for five days. Already we were one day late and progress was very slow. It looked as if we would be lucky to reach Khabarovsk, our destination, in nine days instead of the seven it was supposed to take from Moscow.

A beaming Russian lady who had been watching me leaned forward to pick up my knitting and by pointing the needles in a completely different direction produced identical stitches to mine. Comparing methods kept us occupied for 15 minutes although neither of us shared a word of common language. Her husband spoke a little German.

"Where are you going?" he asked eventually.

"Malaysia," I replied, not surprised to find that this information met with a blank stare. Certainly a route taking me from Britain to Malaysia via the breadth of Siberia, Japan and Thailand was a rather circuitous one.

Over a month later, time was running short when I found myself with only a day to get from Haadyai in southern Thailand to the hotel in Kuala Lumpur where the group of teachers would gather. At the border I asked for a three-year visa. With a quizzical look the immigration authorities eyed my dirty rucksack, advised me to sort this out in Kuala Lumpur and gave me a week.

I had intended to take my time on this final leg to size up good locations for a posting. Three years was a long time and I wanted to make an informed choice. Instead, Malaysia flashed past the bus windows in a blur. Occasionally I spotted schools and wondered if one of them would be mine but by the time I reached Kuala Lumpur all that remained was a confused impression of a hot, humid and very green country with dozens of identical tatty little towns and appallingly dangerous traffic. Travel-stained, exhausted and extremely sweaty, I arrived at the Federal Hotel in Kuala Lumpur to find I had reached it just half an hour before the main group of teachers, coming directly by air from London. I registered my arrival and found my room. The air-conditioned luxury of the hotel took me by surprise. My long, lone journey was over and a new phase in my life was about to begin.

1

The following morning all 80 teachers were called to a plenary session to hear details of the six-week orientation course with which we would begin our stay in Malaysia. Finally we were divided into small groups to tour the immediate vicinity of the hotel and I found myself next to a tall, bearded Scotsman who told me his name was Denis. We discovered a common interest in birds and I promised to lend him the Field Guide which I'd brought with me.

Making contacts was all important, for soon we would be divided into groups of three or four to be given proximate postings. It was important, when our locations were to be so widely scattered, to be relatively close to friends made during the course. Groups formed and reformed. Various combinations of personalities joined for drinks, for dinners, for forays around Kuala Lumpur. Postings were discussed, the pros and cons of various areas disputed. Some wanted to be near Singapore and others near Thailand; some fancied the quiet easy-going Malay east coast, others the more racially mixed west coast. I belonged to the last group and had asked to be posted somewhere in the state of Perak; so, I soon discovered, had Denis. I felt pleased. It would be nice to see more of him and we made plans to go bird-watching together. A week after we arrived in Kuala Lumpur a bus tour of the city was organised for us. Finding Denis alone in the front seat I settled down beside him. We toured the nation's new mosque and the war memorial, we visited the Batu Caves and I borrowed his binoculars to peer at the monkeys and bats. On the way back to the hotel we shared a coconut and agreed to have dinner together that evening.

The Coliseum restaurant, a relic from Malaysia's colonial past, had seen better days. We were both intrigued by its decaying charms — its ancient dark brown paint, slowly revolving fans and antique Chinese waiters in starched white coats. The stiff neatly-patched linen table cloths were stained from the day's meals. We ordered sizzling steaks and were decked in huge white bibs to receive them. We told our life stories over those steaks and when the plates had gone we continued over the patches and the stains ignoring frosty looks from waiters until the place had closed and we had to be asked to leave. As we wandered along the humid streets back towards the hotel, a mass of motorbikes, racing away at the traffic lights, broke into our consciousness and left us clutching each other in fright on a traffic island. We didn't let go. A little orientation romance had begun.

Two days later our postings were unexpectedly announced. Denis was to go to the beautiful town of Taiping and I was to be sent to an insignificant little town 100 miles to the south. Stunned, I tried to make a swap but none of those who had been given Taiping were unhappy or had reason to change. Was our romance to be doomed, separated as we were to be by a three-hour journey on highly treacherous roads?

The main group of teachers was now divided into three sections to continue with the final four weeks of the orientation course, in centres nearer to our postings. At least Denis and I were in the same group and we travelled north to Ipoh together. A fortnight later I visited my town and returned to Ipoh thoroughly depressed. Denis returned from Taiping keener than ever we should both go there. Still no one would consider changing with me.

"Denis, would you fancy swapping towns?" The offer came within a few days of the end of the course from a long-distance runner who had been posted to a town 18 miles from mine, and, finding there was no suitable place to train, had taken a strong fancy to the Taiping Lake Gardens. It seemed to be a solution, if not ideal. Denis's reaction was not, to my mind, as enthusiastic as it could have been. He was most reluctant to leave Taiping but decided to borrow a car for a quick visit to the town on offer.

Rain descended as we left Ipoh and negotiating the unfamiliar roads became a nightmare. Just as we had reached the town, however, it eased off. What stretched before us was one of the most unattractive places I had yet seen. A string of mechanics' yards, piled high with heaps of discarded tyres and engines and stained with puddles of oil lined the approach. A few dilapidated Chinese shop houses and a market area, strewn with vegetable remains and discarded boxes, marked the centre. Then we were through the town and back among the monotonous oil palm plantations which typified the countryside in that area. My heart sank. I didn't dare speak.

"We might as well have a look at Telok Anson," said Denis stoically. That was the nearest town of any size. We drove in silence. Was our budding relationship to end? It was indeed asking a lot to expect Denis to give up Taiping and settle for an ugly little place in the sticks. What if our romance floundered? Three years was a very long time to spend in a place so awful. It was also a long time to spend alone.

Suddenly I was interrupted in my reverie by a huge form flapping across the road just above the car.

"Stop!" I screamed. Denis pulled abruptly off the road.

"What is it?" he shouted, bewildered at my panic as I rummaged frantically for my binoculars.

"Look . . . the birds . . ." I waved across the street at a large three-storey concrete block.

"Good God," he exclaimed and leapt out of the car. Two huge black and white birds with enormous bills were perched on the flat roof of the building. In turn they bounded from the roof, with a flap and a glide reached the nearby tree, and then, follow-my-leader style, returned to the roof. We goggled at them and then at each other.

"Hornbills? Are those hornbills?" we whispered in awe.

The two huge birds seemed attached to springs as with huge bounding leaps they sprang along the roof, one after the other. Then one plucked a fruit from the nearby tree and tossed it in the air for its mate to catch. The other returned it in the same manner. The two birds flirted in front of us for a good half hour while we watched transfixed, attracting not a few curious stares ourselves, from passers-by. It was an omen and as we stood there the storm clouds cleared and the most magnificent, dramatic sunset we were to see in our entire stay in the country shot the sky with scarlet, orange, pink and deep turquoise.

We drove slowly back to Ipoh in the growing darkness.

"I think I'll swap," said Denis. "After all, I wouldn't have to live in the same town as the school. Perhaps I could live with you?"

Denis

Sitting at the back of the MAS DC10 with my legs bunched up against the seat in front, I lifted up the window shutter to look out into the blackness. What was I letting myself in for? Malaysia! After all, apart from a brief mention of rubber production in my secondary school geography class, I hardly knew anything about the place. My train of thought was broken by the person sitting next to me, also a teacher-to-be. He was bringing, he informed me, every volume of the Encyclopaedia Britannica to while away the long, lonely tropical nights. I reached, not for the first time, for my duty-free Glenfiddich. Precious little of it remained by the time we finally landed at Kuala Lumpur airport.

As the last passengers descended on to the tarmac, I finally hoisted myself upright and outside, alcohol oozing from every pore in the humid tropical air. About 50 would-be Malaysian school teachers were shepherded through passport control and customs and on to buses with military efficiency. A teacher who had already spent some time in Malaysia then gave a running commentary on the invisible scenery as we sped into the city in the darkness. "Microcosm of Malaysia", I heard, as imaginary rubber estates gave way to unseen oil palm plantations. Never mind, I was already feeling cosier in the protective arms of our organisation — the Centre For British Teachers. I looked around the bus. Were there any people, male or female, who looked like potential friends? Tired faces looked back at me with glazed eyes.

An air-conditioned bus to an air-conditioned hotel in the heart of Kuala Lumpur was hardly the introduction to Malaysia that I expected. Groups of administrators welcomed us and ushered us into lifts and to rooms which were to be shared by two teachers. In general, single men were stuck together in dingy back rooms which looked on to the ventilator shaft. Waking up in the morning to darkness and the freezing whirr of the air-con was not how I had envisaged tropical mornings through the writings of Somerset Maugham and Anthony Burgess.

This was the orientation course where I learned that words like 'plenary' and 'de-briefing' were actually used in real life. The six-week orientation was to prepare us for the idiosyncracies of Malaysia and its education system as well as teach us a bit of the Malay language. We also had to decide, most importantly, which part of the country we wanted to spend the next three years in − a decision to be made within the first two weeks! Establishing contacts with teachers of like minds as quickly as possible became a priority.

I got to know Stella over the frequent coffee breaks by the hotel swimming pool. She was a bird-watcher and wanted to be near to the Cameron Highlands. I too was keen on birds but had heard that Taiping was the nicest town in Malaysia. As posting day approached the debate over which were the best places to live increased. Most of my little group of new-found friends had settled on the states of Perak and Penang. So far so good. But when the realisation dawned that something more than ornithological compatibility was growing between Stella and myself, it was too late. She had got her posting near to the Cameron Highlands at a town on the main north-south trunk road and I had been sent to a school outside Taiping. We were crestfallen. Three hours' drive on a suicidal race track between towns would surely destroy our nascent relationship.

All teachers now went to the second part of the orientation course in the areas of Malaysia where they had chosen to live. For the next few weeks in Ipoh we tried desperately to get Stella a posting in Taiping which she now agreed was a far more attractive proposition than the one she'd been given. Nobody wanted to leave Taiping but someone was happy to give me his posting in southern Perak only 18 miles from Stella.

To lose my plum posting on account of such a new relationship was a major decision to make and at least required a visit to the area to check it out. As we drove through the town where my future school might be, my heart sank. Litter, mangy dogs and rusty machinery from the many run down repair shops lined the dirty main street. It was a typical Malaysian 'cowboy town' with no apparent saving graces.

Stella sensed my mood and we drove in silence to nearby Telok Anson to view prospective accommodation. It's easy in retrospect to see what happened there as an omen but at the time it was simply the beautiful courtship display of two birds. On top of a modern building in the centre of the town sat a pair of pied hornbills caressing each other's bills and throwing fruit in the air for each other to catch − something we never saw again, least of all in an urban setting. We watched for a long time and it was, undoubtedly, those birds which influenced me when I made my decision to agree to the posting transfer.

Our gamble paid off. We grew increasingly close to each other and increasingly fond of the little community we found ourselves living in. A year later we decided to get married (the wedding is described at the end of 'Marriages') and two years after the hornbill sighting we had our own little baby boy.

2

Kampong and Town

Our arrival in the kampong, or Malay 'village', where we were to live for the next three years caused considerable excitement. Our landlord and his family had camped in the house overnight to be sure they could greet us the following morning. Neighbours peered unabashed from windows, doors and gateways as our taxi drove up. Europeans were normally only seen in the small town if they stopped for petrol or a quick meal on their way between Kuala Lumpur and Penang. None stopped for longer, none visited the kampong some distance from the town and certainly none had ever come to live there.

Our new house was not at all what we had visualised. Everywhere in Malaysia we had seen typical, stilted, wooden houses, surrounded by luxuriant vegetation; tall, gracefully bending coconut palms, bright, huge-leafed banana plants, dark mango trees and abundant, decorative bushes. Our dream was to live like that, in the cool, quiet shade of the verdant, tropical environment.

The reality which faced us now was a square concrete box with bare cement floors, in a compound of dusty grey gravel and builders' rubble surrounded by barbed wire, which for a long time we nicknamed, because of its utilitarian appearance, "the power station". It was built on a former tin mine. The methods of extraction in Malaysia are responsible for large tracts of totally unproductive land. The tin is simply washed out of the soil along with all nutrients leaving a sterile gravel on which even secondary growth takes many years to develop. Even after 20 years the soil of our garden was useless for much other than weeds.

We tried politely to hide our disappointment and, removing our shoes, stepped inside. Our landlord, a very friendly and, we were to realise later, an unusually energetic Malay, spoke no English. Communication was limited so, with effusive expressions of friendship on each side, the family soon packed themselves into their car and drove off.

Left to ourselves we started clearing up the house and discussing what furniture was most immediately necessary. Before long, however, the shuffle of ubiquitous rubber flip-flops announced the arrival of visitors. There was much unseen cackling until one brown face peered, smiling, round the door followed by another and then another. Flip-flops having been shed, these ample faces were joined by suitably generous figures. Several enormous women, having negotiated the door, followed one another uninvited into the living room and, beaming, settled themselves in a semicircle on the concrete floor. After them poured a stream of whispering children of all ages, subdued and unsmiling, examining us with wide, dark eyes as they nestled close to their respective mothers, several almost disappearing under the maternal plumage. Anxious to make a good start in the kampong we laboured to stretch our few words and phrases to a conversation. Our visitors beamed on, discussing us openly among themselves.

Then with a common impulse they hoisted themselves to their feet and, chattering their way with tiny shrieks and giggles into their shoes, waddled off down the garden path.

As that shift left, the next arrived. Evidently word had got round that the *orang putih* (white people) were on show. A young man pushed his way through the mob of departing children and, urging his fellows to follow, plonked himself down authoritatively.

"These are my friends," he said. Since we didn't know him this seemed a little irrelevant but we did our best to maintain our smiles and chit chat. Visitations kept us busy for most of the day.

Early next morning, we had just started on our cleaning operations for the umpteenth time when the landlord reappeared with an electrician and hanger-on to fix the lights. This served as an excuse for the entire neighbourhood to re-tour our house; so in they all trooped and, more confident now, strutted about the place examining the few pieces of furniture we had managed to buy. Young-man-down-the-road acted as guide for a few more of his peers. Children swarmed through the rooms. Several decided to investigate the contents of our fridge no doubt hoping for a titillating view of the forbidden pork. Others, roaming the garden, peered through the windows. Everywhere enquiring faces popped into sight.

Unprepared for this barrage, our smiles wearied and our hearts sank; although keen to have friendly neighbours, we valued our privacy. How would it be possible to live here as public property, constantly under the uninvited gaze of one curiosity seeker or another? How could we hint to such amiable people that as Europeans we liked to choose our times for socialising?

Happily, however, the situation resolved itself. The enthusiastic welcome tailed off and we became, however odd, part of the life of the kampong. Our comings and goings, our habits and our friends were kept under constant surveillance, but only the arrival of our baby boy at the end of the second year and the selling of our furniture before we left attracted quite the same crowds.

* * *

Life in the kampong was peaceful. Mornings started early, in time for pre-dawn prayers at 5.45 a.m. These early hours of the day were always the best. The temperature was refreshingly cool. Rain rarely fell in the morning. The best days began clear and calm and after the rapid dawn, the sun rose quickly casting a brilliant light which made the dullest scenes sparkle with beauty. Birds and animals were busy, chickens scratching, bulbuls and sparrows twittering, goats foraging before the heat drove them under cover. Herds of great black buffaloes with fierce expressions and docile temperaments ambled around the kampong under the watchful eye of their turbanned Sikh owners. Later they would retire from the heat to the nearby river to loll, submerged but for their heads, until hunger struck once more.

By nine or ten o'clock the freshness had gone and our skins were already sticky with sweat. Washing fluttered on fences in the now scorching sun. Marketing and cleaning finished, cooking occupied the women, pestles ringing out in mortars as spices were ground for the midday meal. By three o'clock in the afternoon the kampong fell silent as the inhabitants snoozed away the hottest and most enervating time of the day.

We were all, perhaps, told in our school geography lessons that rain in the tropics falls with clockwork regularity every evening. This is not true. Sometimes a month or even longer would pass in the 'summer' without a decent shower, but on the ideal day the late afternoon calm would be suddenly interrupted by a rushing wind. Roofs would rattle, doors slam and the tousled fronds of the distant coconut palms would sway frenziedly as the storm headed towards us. Bloated black clouds would sweep down from the mountains streaked with flashes of lightning. Finally the rain could be heard approaching, hammering on the zinc roofs of the neighbours' houses seconds before it reached ours. For a brief instant it would be dry on one side of our house while rain lashed the other. Then we were engulfed in torrents. Conversations were impossible and radios inaudible as the rain thundered down. Sheets of water poured out of the gutters and buckets left outside overflowed within minutes. Drains swirled, flowers were flattened and water flooded in under the doors. Lightning flashed and cracked simultaneously. Thunder exploded over our heads. Five times our house was struck and once a nearby wooden house was burned to the ground.

The storm would leave as suddenly as it had come, usually within an hour. As the retreating clouds carried the rain off elsewhere the children would appear, splashing in the puddles, pedalling their bicycles through the flooded kampong and trying to catch prawns in the now torrential streams. The evening cool would bring the kampong dwellers, their work done, out to cluster, chatting and cackling, babies in arms. Men ambled about on bicycles so slowly they could scarcely maintain their balance, babies and children clinging on fore and aft.

Our neighbours were relaxed. They never appeared to fret or hurry. They never seemed anxious. They never ran for buses or got flustered but then there was never any need to rush. Not much was attempted beyond the basics of life. Our neighbours never went to cinemas, dances or exhibitions. They had no evening classes to attend, and seldom gave parties beyond those dictated by the calendar of celebrations. They rarely travelled unnecessarily or read books. The men in the evening most often attended the mosque. For many the highlight of the evening was a Malay drama on TV. They had, in fact, a remarkable ability to do nothing. They could sit totally idle for hours, a state which would drive even the most easy-going westerner to activity of some sort. Young men, waiting months and even years to be given a government job, knew nothing of the frustrations of unemployment.

They simply waited patiently and unhurriedly for fate to play its next card. Their lives, by western standards, were horrifically dull, their demeanour enviably relaxed.

Isabella Bird, a visitor to Malaysia 100 years before us, described thus the favourite wife of the Sultan of Selangor; "our conversation was not brilliant and the Sultana looked to me as if she had attained nirvana and had neither ideas nor the consciousness of the absence of ideas." Judged by these criteria, many of our neighbours lived similarly in a state of nirvana.

Sir Frank Swettenham, however, a prominent British administrator during the final thirty years of the 19th century, led us to look for more. He wrote of Malay women that they could be characterised by .... "powers of intelligent conversation, quickness in repartee, a strong sense of humour and an instant appreciation of the real meaning of those hidden sayings which are hardly ever absent from their conversations. . . ."

"We Malays say . . . ," began our neighbour one morning, rocking our new-born son next to her enormous bosom. We pricked up our ears hoping for some gems. "When the baby sleeps," she continued, "we must work."

On spotting his naked torso in the 90 degree heat one afternoon she began again.

"We Malays say . . . ," Again we held our breaths. "Baby cannot like this – will catch cold."

Was something lost in the translation? We doubted it. With the destruction of their traditional way of life and the introduction of western ways something fragile seemed to have crumbled without being replaced by anything of substance. The clever *pantuns* or poem-like proverbs enthused about by early writers have not given way to the analytical approach which characterises western thinking. Instead only the most tangible and most mediocre aspects of western culture have been adopted. Tuneless Malay versions of western pop songs blare from Japanese cassette players. TVs in every house offer a backdrop of largely American soap operas – 'Dallas,' 'Chips,' 'Charlie's Angels', etc. etc., the meagre subtitles describing the action without translating the dialogue which remains unintelligible to most Malays. Nonetheless the 'box' dominates, stifling conversation, suppressing family interaction.

The sudden introduction of consumerism to this traditionally delicately-mannered people, until recently innocent of a cash economy, was also responsible for a number of unattractive traits. We never quite came to terms with the Malay attitude to money. Every piece of furniture we bought for the house prompted an examination and the same demand – "*Berapa*? (how much?)" This one word became a source of great irritation to us. Were they interested in how much extra the white folks had had to pay? Or was it merely a conversational gambit much as the state of the weather would be in Britain?

"How much?" asked our neighbour stopping to chat on her evening stroll, pointing over the fence to a potted plant. It had been grown from a cutting. "Nothing."

She paused, stymied, and pondered her next move. "The pot?" Her face brightened as she indicated the small, everyday earthern-ware pot from the local sundry shop. "*Berapa?*"

"Fifty cents."

"You give me when you leave?" was her instant response. She was an unashamedly acquisitive woman and along with her neighbours had decided exactly which of our belongings she would bid for three years hence when we made our exit.

One evening we proudly showed our landlord some orchid flowers which we'd produced, once more from a cutting. "*Mahal* (expensive!)" he exclaimed. The flower had again cost nothing to produce but would have cost quite a lot in the market. This was simply his way of complimenting our flower.

When replying to questions about salaries we dodged and evaded. We knew that we earned more than the average local teachers but were reluctant to admit it. We wanted to appear as equals, not as the privileged expatriates. If we told them we felt sure it would lead to resentment though we later realised that, owing to our qualifications and experience, they expected us to earn a lot more.

Their forthright questions were often offensive to our sophisticated western sensibilities, developed over centuries of intercourse with a money economy and garnished with such long-winded preambles as "I hope you don't mind me asking but I was wondering. . . .". In other matters, however, we were just as oblivious to their particular sensibilities and doubtless offended them unknowingly on many occasions. We knew not to eat with our left hands and to remove our shoes before entering a house. It took time, however, to realise we should not point to a person with the outstretched index finger but with the thumb and it took practice to adopt their limp handshake or their method for politely crossing a crowded room. When wishing to do so a person must bend at the waist and, while stretching the open palm of the right hand almost to the floor, scuttle apologetically across the room.

Although curious about our day to day activities, our neighbours showed a remarkable lack of interest in us beyond our Malaysian context. They rarely asked us anything about Britain, our families, what we had done before we came to Malaysia, why we had chosen to come or other countries we had visited. They were remarkably parochial. Even those who had travelled abroad seemed more struck by problems of climate and food than by new sights and experiences. Nearly every conversation was related sooner or later back to Malaysia: "How do you find Malaysia?" was the eager question asked ad infinitum. Perhaps this introversion was merely the inability of a contented home-loving people to project themselves beyond their own environment or perhaps it was the result of belonging to a proud new nation, barely 25 years old, constantly bombarded with government propaganda aimed at building a national consciousness among the disparate races.

* * *

The town, two miles from our house, contained few Malays. They prefer the peace and quiet of their small communities and for the most part avoid the commercial activities of the towns. The Chinese dominated here, running the market and the shops, the garages and restaurants. Almost all the business of the town was in their hands although there were a few Indian-owned shops, as readily recognisable by the aroma of spices as by the curlicued script of their Tamil signboards.

Most of the inhabitants lived in rows of link houses close to the centre. These areas reflected well the convivial nature of Chinese society. Chinese teachers often asked us if we would not like to move into town but we never shared their ability to live and sleep through the decibel level created by the clamorous tones of Chinese dialects, screaming children, blaring TVs, radios, stereos and videos and the barking of dogs which conducted their nightly feuds unhindered in the streets.

Situated on the main Kuala Lumpur to Penang highway, the town was bisected by an almost continuous, racing cavalcade of traffic; laden timber trucks, oil palm tankers, express buses, speeding taxis and cars which scarcely noticed its existence and certainly accorded it hardly a dip of the speedometer. It was like so many of the small towns on that route. The Chinese shophouses lined the main street, living quarters above the shops projecting over and shading the pavement, supported by pillars thickly embossed with Chinese characters. Mounds of discarded bits of machinery surrounded garages, rubble collected in neglected corners and oil clogged the roadside drains — rubbish, so pervasive in Malaysian towns, it eventually becomes invisible.

The speciality of the area dangled from racks on the main street, an inducement for aficionados to halt in their headlong dash north or south. Known as *petai* the long green pods were collected from the local forest. Inside nestled fat beans, bitter and foul-tasting, which, due to their peculiar chemical make up, should be washed down with glasses of salted water.

The restaurants of the town also beckoned to the traveller. A convenient half-way halt they did a brisk trade but we rarely ate in them. It was a bit off-putting to pass by the rear of these establishments and observe the dirty dishes being washed in the drain or steeped in buckets providing nourishment for the town's stray dogs.

Also hidden from the view of the highway users was the market which bustled from dawn each morning with sellers and buyers of fish, vegetables and fruit, the canopied pork market set well aside from the main area to spare the sensibilities of the Malays. Most of the stalls were Chinese and a few Indian, while a lone Malay sold religiously acceptable beef. Behind, chickens sulked in cages awaiting the moment of doom when, their throats absent-mindedly slashed, they would flap their last in a blood-soaked basket and be delivered plucked and warm, complete with disdainful heads and scrubbed feet, delicacies for which we never did develop an appetite.

The crowded sundry shops provided our other needs. Cheap plastic goods from China dangled thickly from the ceiling. The floors were littered with sacks of rice, cans of paraffin, baskets of charcoal and mounds of coconuts. Here we bought our spices, not in neatly labelled bottles but from dusty boxes and barrels containing heaps of seeds and powders sold by the handful and wrapped in newspaper. Identification was often difficult for us and on occasions puzzled shopkeepers, unable to understand what we wanted, called passers-by of various races in from the street to help. Discussion was intense, the search determined and once even the postman was diverted from his rounds to give advice.

Thursday was the day when a travelling market sprawled its maze of stalls over a patch of wasteland. The displays of synthetic materials, cassettes, sarongs and prayer mats were mundane enough but on the fringes would appear vendors of a more exotic kind. A Buddhist monk with a display of tarot cards, magic stones and figurines would sit cross-legged, chanting, lighting incense and authoritatively turning cards to disclose the secrets of his customers' futures. Snake charmers or dancing bears drew crowds to medicine sellers or, if they lacked such attractions, vividly coloured and horrific photographs of skin diseases and haemorrhoids served to illustrate their claims.

Traditional Chinese medicines were also to be found in the local apothecary's. Dried stags' horns, preserved turtles, herbs, roots and powders, colourful boxes with Chinese inscriptions and oddly shaped bottles of potions jostled with aspirins and antiseptics, Milk of Magnesia and sticking plasters.

We were never very sure how the townspeople felt about us. Certainly after the enthusiastic inquisitiveness of our neighbours, the apparent total lack of interest displayed by the Chinese shopkeepers came as rather a shock. In the newspaper shop, however, we discovered that we were referred to as "red-haired devil schoolteachers" for that was what was scribbled in Chinese characters at the top of our daily paper, 'red-haired devil' being the Chinese term for foreigners, coined in the age when the first Europeans arrived in China and preserved forever in their ideographic script.

The town was studded with places of worship catering for the variety of beliefs in this diverse community. At each end were mosques for the Malays, places of quiet design built before the spate of flamboyant, onion-domed, government subsidised constructions which have sprung up in other towns. The Hindu temple in the centre of town typified the ornate south-Indian style. Clustered around the exterior dome and on the facade, a fanciful collection of gaudily painted plaster statues represented a mere fraction of the vast Hindu pantheon, the elephant god, Ganesh, being the most prominent as the temple was dedicated to him. Inside, the altar featured another garlanded black stone statue of him, while a cow, on a pedestal of pastel tiles, faced him in homage from under its burden of freshly strewn petals.

Across the road the Sikh community worshipped in a temple less remarkable for its plain, utilitarian appearance than for its priest, a hugely-bearded, fierce-looking man recently imported from India. Dressed in long white robes, his head cocooned in an immense white turban, a curved dagger hanging from a dark blue sash, he was a striking sight strolling around the town, staff in hand. For a long time, before we were introduced to him, he would stare at us with as much curiosity as we looked at him but after our meeting we were always greeted with a broad smile, hands held palms together in the Indian form of salutation.

The Chinese temple was no less decorative than the Hindu one. Two dragons pranced along the ridge of the tilted roof and more coiled around the interior pillars. Two large gilded statues of Emperor gods sat enthroned on the altar behind numerous huge incense burners constantly spiked with smoking joss sticks, the distinctive smell of which permeated the entire area. Outside, two ornately panelled red incinerators stood for the disposal of burning joss papers. There were always a few people to be seen saying their prayers, several burning incense sticks held between their pressed palms and dipped in ritualistic fashion towards the alter before being implanted in the burners.

A roofed area in front of the temple provided the local children with a playground for most of the year. Four weeks before the Chinese New Year, however, it was transformed by the arrival of a travelling Chinese opera company. Every afternoon and evening for two weeks they would emerge on to the stage, faces grotesquely painted, garbed in the brightest of colours, the richest of brocades and the most elaborate of costumes and head-dresses, sequins glittering in the footlights, to perform with high-pitched cater-wauling, declamations, shrieks and antics to the accompaniment of clashing cymbals, drums, wood blocks and a two-stringed 'violin'. Incense, hundreds of small sticks, several smouldering five-foot columns and dozens of coils three feet in diameter each with a prayer on paper attached to the centre, filled the temple with a choking smoke during the show. Constructed near the altar, paper figures of the resident deities on horseback as well as a giant paper Buddha had sumptuous feasts with numerous bowls of assorted food laid out before them.

Sadly this strange and marvellous spectacle is rapidly losing popularity as TV and video take over. Nevertheless, few Chinese in the town would not drop by to savour the atmosphere for at least part of the three-hour performance, bringing the older people a nostalgic memory of the land they left as youngsters and their children a taste of the country they will probably never be able to see.

3

Races and Parties

W e grew attached to our little house. Papaya trees, orange flowering weeds, wild guava trees and potted bougainvillaeas eventually softened its power station aspect. Nearby ponds, rivers and bushes provided us with a variety of walks and a good introduction to the local birds. Building on the area was sparse and seemed unplanned, being limited to about a dozen houses. There was plenty of open land and we enjoyed the feeling of space. Occasionally new houses were built on apparently random spots and left vacant.

Towards the end of our stay, however, there was an unprecedented spate of activity. Suddenly bulldozers appeared to clear areas of weeds and bushes, lorries arrived with loads of bricks, sand and timber. Groups of people could be seen taking a sudden interest in the barren land, hammering in pegs, stretching lines and discussing plans. Builders arrived, bricks were laid and roofs erected. An unaccustomed sound of hammering and banging echoed around the kampong.

'What is going on?" we enquired of our neighbours.

As usual they knew all the details. The whole area, which we had for three years thought to be unclaimed waste land had in fact, seven years previously, been divided into plots and sold for the tiny sum of M$300* to cover surveying fees. Most of the owners had bought and not developed them and now had been told that if they had nothing built within three months they would have their plots reclaimed and resold by the government. Hence the frantic building activity.

The real value of the land was revealed by the wheelings and dealings of a local Indian. He bought one of the plots of land beside our house from the Malay owner for M$6,000 intending to build on it himself. The deal was conducted through a lawyer and a deed of sale legally drawn up. The land was then transferred but the agreement had to be ratified at the Land Office where it was refused; so the Indian found himself with a piece of land which he had paid for but could not legally own. The man had simply been refused permission to build because he was an Indian. The area where we rented our house consisted of land reserved for Malays only, the result of government discrimination in their favour.

Although the small number of aborigines (Orang Asli) have been in the country much longer, the Malays are recognised officially as the chief indigenous racial group, this despite the fact that a great many of them have parents and grandparents who came from Indonesia. Indeed, in 1940 it was estimated that out of 2,300,000 'Malays' in the country over 50 per cent were actually Muslim, Malay-speaking immigrants. The rest of the population was composed of Chinese and Indians, referred to collectively as non-Malays.

When the British first began to take control of the peninsula in the late

*US$ = M$2.50 approx.

19th century, there was already a large number of Chinese living there. They had spilled out from their overcrowded and poverty-stricken native land, mostly from the south-eastern provinces of China, especially Kwangtung and Fukien, speaking principally the local dialects of Cantonese and Hokkien, They came in great numbers to work the mines with the intention of returning to China with their savings. Most never did but instead stayed in Malaya, the more successful ones expanding their role to that of shop-keepers, merchants and traders.

The resident Malays were not used to competing for their livelihood. Coconuts, fruit and fish were readily available. Crops of rice could be grown once or twice a year. Their population was small, food was abundant and effort was largely unnecessary as was a need to trade. In the time of the British the Malays saw no reason for seeking wage labour so the British encouraged the Chinese immigrants. Only they were willing to work the mines or to clear the land for plantations in return for cash.

From the turn of the century onwards Indians, particularly Tamils but also from the Telegu and Malayalee linguistic areas of south India, were encouraged by the British to leave their impoverished lands to provide a docile and hardworking labour force in railway construction and as rubber tappers in the expanding estates. In addition to labourers there was a con-siderable Indian and Ceylonese Tamil 'white collar' class employed in clerical work. The smaller number of northern Indians who came included Sikhs and a few Bengalis.

By the time of independence in 1957 the non-Malays made up almost half of the population with 48.5 per cent, approximately 10 per cent being Indians. Malays numbered only 49.8 per cent. But even these statistics hide the true impact of the non-Malays, particularly the Chinese who, due to a diligence and competitiveness heightened by hardship and coupled with a pecuniary approach to life, controlled large sections of the economy. In addition, as well as the legendary secret societies based on common origin in districts of China, they had a remarkable facility for organising themselves into trade associations to further business interests. Without curbs the Chinese could almost completely dominate the Malays economically.

It was this which frightened the Malays. They bargained long and hard with the British before a compromise was reached. The non-Malays were to be given access to citizenship, those born after independence gaining it automatically, in exchange for which the Malays were to enjoy political dominance and recognition of their 'special rights'.

An uneasy peace was maintained between the communities for 12 years aided by the natural segregation of the races, the Malays mainly in the rural areas, the Chinese in the towns. In 1969, however, the superficial harmony was shattered. The largely Chinese opposition parties DAP and Gerakan gained, for the first time, the same number of electoral seats as the Malay-dominated government alliance in the state of Selangor, including the federal capital, Kuala Lumpur. Their provocative victory march incensed the Malays, who, *en masse*, ran amok. No one knows how many were killed but the figures were estimated in hundreds. What became clearly apparent, however, was that if the country was not to split apart at the seams with racial violence, the standard of living of the Malays would have to be raised. They were no longer content to live the leisurely life of the kampong if it entailed a comparative poverty. They saw themselves being left behind as the country developed, rapidly losing ground to the non-Malays. What the Chinese had, they felt, should by rights be theirs and the government recognised it was ultimately better to give it to them than for jealousy to inflame racial hatred. In order to reassure the Malays their 'special rights' were re-stated and reinforced.

These special rights were granted early on by the British who appreciated the vulnerability of the Malays and were expanded in the early 1970s in the aftermath of the race riots. At present they include land reserved solely for Malay use, as in our kampong, a quota of licences for certain businesses and three out of four government appointments, with civil servants eligible for low interest loans. There are also special quotas for Malays in universities and colleges. At least 70 per cent of places are reserved for them along with scholarships and educational grants. In addition Malays benefit from sole access to government shares. The aim is for Malays to own at least 30 per cent of the country's economic wealth by 1990. In the early 1970s they controlled only 2 per cent; at present it is about 18 per cent although this figure is slightly misleading in that the wealth is held largely by trust agencies created and funded by the government rather than through individual Malay initiative. (It must be pointed out, however, that foreign ownership at the time of independence amounted to over 60 per cent and even today it is over 30 per cent.)

Those who qualify for these special privileges are known as *bumiputeras* – *bumi* meaning earth and *putera* meaning prince. This is more prosaically translated as 'sons of the soil'. The term *bumiputera* is supposed to apply to the indigenous people including the Orang Asli but also often applies to first and second generation Muslim immigrants who use Malay as their first language. This has led to a situation where Malays who have recently immigrated from Indonesia can be given rights over Chinese whose families have been in the country for a lot longer.

Everything in Malaysia, we found, revolved around race. It was an often unconscious but perpetual preoccupation and determined every dealing every Malaysian had with every other. Resentment was rife but overt expression of it illegal. The *Rukunegara*, a formal statement of national ideology drawn up in 1970, upheld equality for all races and made it illegal to offend the sensitivities of any group. Many topics are termed 'sensitive subjects'. It is an offence to question openly the special privileges of the Malays and the powers of the Malay rulers, the position of Islam as the national religion and Malay as the national language. Anyone who does so can be locked up under the terms of the ISA (Internal Security Act) as a threat to national security.

Malaysian leaders refer to their political system as a controlled democracy where parliamentary elections are held every five years on the British model. There are, however, a lot more thinly populated rural Malay constituencies than populous urban Chinese ones and Malays have a far greater number of MPs in relation to their total population than the non-Malays. Additionally, the Chinese and Indians are given much more to political in-fighting than the Malays who traditionally have a greater loyalty to their leaders. Thus in spite of divisions created by Islamic fundamentalists the government is generally returned to power with a big majority.

Politically, one belongs to one's skin. The founder of the Malay party UMNO (United Malay National Organisation) Dato' Onn Ja'afar tried to start a multi-racial party in the early 1950s but he was much too far ahead of his time and it failed. It is actually impossible for an individual to join the 'wrong' communal political Party. A Malay cannot join the MCA (Malaysian Chinese Association) and even a Ceylonese Tamil cannot become a member of the MIC (Malaysian Indian Congress). He must adhere to the non-political Jaffna Society. This situation dates back to the post-war pre-independence period when each powerful racial group sought to maximise its communal advantage over the other. This inevitably exacerbated racial differences. Having pushed for what they regarded as their own essential ethnic rights, all three major communal parties eventually appreciated the need to join forces. Until the 1969 riots they were known as the Alliance and subsequently (and still today) as the National Front or Barisan Nasional, comprising UMNO as the big brother with the MCA and Gerakan (formerly in opposition) for the Chinese, the MIC for the Indians plus component parties of Sabah and Sarawak. All these latter parties feel that there is more advantage to be gained working with UMNO. The major opposition parties are the DAP (Democratic Action Party) a non-communal party consisting of largely Chinese members and PAS the Pan Islamic National Party of Malay fundamentalists.

The communal nature of political parties, however, has tended to mask class divisions. The NEP (New Economic Policy) which implemented 'positive discrimination' in the early 1970s, while succeeding to a certain extent in its aim of creating a Malay urban middle class, has more effectively produced a large number of very wealthy Malays particularly in the public sector (to parallel the Chinese in the private sector) who are labelled by the cynical as *UMNOputeras*. On the other hand poverty in the community as a whole appears to be on the increase rather than the decrease.

In 1980 29.2 per cent were considered to be below the official poverty line while the figure stood at 30.3 per cent in 1983.

These statistics, of course, do not differentiate between the Malays and the non-Malays, who suffer discrimination merely because of racial links with their more prosperous cousins. However, the fact of poverty in the country tends to be underplayed and it could be argued that ethnic differences are successfully used to distract attention from latent class interests as the elites of each community continue quietly to improve their economic position with little tangible regard for the poor. Some concerned Malaysians have suggested that a National Economic Policy be implemented after 1990 (the date that special advantages to the Malays are supposed to cease) to improve the position of all poor Malaysians irrespective of race. This seems unlikely as the government would find it difficult to take away advantages which most Malays, (even if they don't make use of them) accept as their right.

As mentioned earlier, the government can use the threat of the ISA to stifle any criticism which it considers not in the national interest and indeed many people are in detention without trial. Both the DAP and PAS as well as certain newspapers have this sword of Damocles occasionally waggled over their heads. Newspaper comment, in particular, is therefore heavily self-censored and Malaysians in general, aware of the sensitive nature of political and religious issues do not discuss them openly.

As Europeans, we had no obvious allegiances so we heard many sides of the political story particularly the interminable grumbles of the non-*bumiputeras*. Most Malaysians, nevertheless, realise they are living with a potentially volatile situation and must be flexible for all to survive. The traditional reticence of the Asian character in general, a dislike of open conflict and the shocking lesson of 1969 together with the subsequent legislation all help to maintain a certain harmony in spite of deep differences, prejudices and loyalties. Even many of the non-*bumiputeras* realise they must give up some of their economic dominance in order to gain social stability. As one Chinese man put it, "as long as they have their Hondas they are less likely to smash up my Mercedes!" The resulting tolerance, however, could unfortunately most often be better described as avoidance and the races remain largely ignorant of and uninterested in each other. Contacts between Malays and non-Malays we found to be almost always very superficial. However, while we were in the country the relative harmony, aided by overall economic growth, was maintained.

4

Islam

ll Malays are, by definition, Muslims. They are subject not only to the civil laws of the country which cover all races but also to the *syaria* or Islamic religious laws with their own separate courts, punishments and religious police. Apostasy is forbidden. We knew of a Malay woman who, having married an Australian, had renounced her faith and become a Christian. On a visit to relatives in Malaysia she was arrested by the religious police, tried and imprisoned. On the whole, however, the Malays accept the laws of Islam and if they contravene them do so discreetly.

The main obligations for Muslims are to believe there is no God but Allah with Mohammed as his prophet, to pray five times a day, to observe the fasting month of Ramadan (in Malay called Bulan Puasa) each year and, if possible, to make the pilgrimage to Mecca. The fifth obligation is to pay a voluntary religious tax called *zakat*, although it is difficult to say how often this is done.

The mosque is an important centre and symbol for the Malays. Every town has at least one, whether small or large, old and picturesque or brand new and grandiose. A special feature of Malaysian life is the haunting call to prayer, broadcast five times a day from the loudspeakers on the minarets. Even schools have separate *suraus* or praying rooms for Muslim teachers and school children which they sometimes visit in preference to attending classes.

The evening prayers of the day seem to be the most important ones, the ululating tones of "Allahu Akbar" adding a magical serenity to the rapidly gathering dusk. Non-Muslim television viewers, however, are not so entranced when the climax of their favourite television programme is abruptly interrupted by the evening prayer, transcribed in attractive but unintelligible Arabic script.

Only on Fridays, the day chosen by God in the Koran, are Muslim men required to attend the mosque and in some Malaysian states Friday and Saturday constitute the weekend with work beginning again on Sunday. In the more urbanised, and consequently Chinese states, Saturday and Sunday are the free days and on Friday government offices close between 12 noon and 2.30 p.m. Morning sessions at schools stop early and the afternoon sessions begin late. For many it is virtually a half day as crowds of men dressed in humble sarongs, crocheted caps or *songkoks*, the stiff black national hat, converge on the mosques. There, they face kiblah (the direction of Mecca), and perform together the Islamic prayer ritual or 'bendings', so called because each part of the ritual is marked by a change of position.

Women pray at home and in the evening, through an unshut louvre, we would occasionally catch a glimpse of our neighbours, swathed in white from head to foot preparing to prostrate themselves to Allah. Muslims never seem to be at all self-conscious while praying. On a train in Thailand once, we watched amazed as the Malay woman in front of us donned her white robes, smoothed out her prayer mat on the seat and proceeded to pray towards Mecca, precision in this being somewhat difficult as the train was negotiating a series of bends. The woman's sister, meanwhile, clad in tight jeans and T-shirt, head uncovered, continued to chat to us about her smuggling activities between Thailand and Malaysia, an undertaking in which, on this occasion, her sister had joined her. Another time, during a school trip to the Cameron Highlands the Malay teachers, apparently unconcerned by the presence of non-Muslims in the same dormitory, arose before dawn, unrolled their prayer mats and lined up facing the wall for 15 minutes of silent prostrations. Perhaps this lack of self-consciousness is because they are performing an obligatory act most often in the company of others. For western Christians, because prayer is a choice and not a compulsion, it arouses a degree of self-consciousness whether it be pride or embarrassment.

Although Muslim men are permitted up to four wives at a time (while other Malaysians must be monogamous), sex outside marriage is strictly forbidden. The law covering this prohibits even 'close proximity'. Known as *khalwat*, it keeps the religious police particularly busy. They sweep down on courting couples in parks and on beaches and break into hotel rooms acting on tip-offs. When we were in Malaysia, some odd cases came to court and were reported in the papers. A divorced couple were caught having a reunion and charged. A man and woman who had been living together for five years and had two children were each sent to prison for six months with no mention of the fate of their offspring. In another tragic case a young girl of 21 was raped by her stepfather. Although threatened by him she eventually plucked up enough courage to report it but instead of receiving help and sympathy, she was accused of *khalwat* and, already several months pregnant from the ordeal, imprisoned for six months during which time she gave birth on the cell floor.

By contrast, the most amusing statement on *khalwat* which we read about was of a male driving instructor, on the more religiously strict east coast, who was accused of the crime of *khalwat* along with his female student. Women, the judge decreed, when unrelated to male companions in a car, should always sit in the back. This obviously caused concern to women learners in the town as there were no female instructors and the Kelantan Driving Instructors' Association chairman urged the State Religious Department "to clarify whether women learner drivers sitting next to instructors could be arrested for *khalwat*."

Pork eating, of course, is also forbidden for Muslims and in fact all meat they do eat must be halal. This means the person who slaughters it must face towards Mecca and say a swift prayer at the moment of death. This prohibition is perhaps one of the most divisive in the multi-racial society of Malaysia, for mixed groups can only eat in a Malay house or in the few halal restaurants (most restaurants being Chinese), and as a consequence rarely share one of life's most sociable acts. Even cooking utensils which have been used for *haram* (forbidden or non-halal) food are considered unclean and should be ritually scrubbed seven times with sand and water before they are purified. This means even fish or vegetables cannot be eaten by Malays in a Chinese restaurant that serves pork and caused our neighbours embarrassment when we pressed our home-made biscuits and cakes on them – they knew we ate pork at home although we tried to keep it out of sight in their presence.

As the government made constant attempts to placate the resurgent Islamic trends within the country its decrees affecting all races acquired an increasingly Islamic flavour. Kissing was banned in public as a corrupt western import although it wasn't known whether hordes of religious secret police would be waiting at airports to pounce on unsuspecting families bidding farewell or welcome to friends and relatives. Hotels and shops were obliged to operate separate fridges for halal and non-halal foodstuffs. In addition, restaurants which served both types of food had to have separate cooking and eating areas. Advertisements for non-halal goods on television were banned. While producing a certificate was relatively easy for halal food manufacturers, makers of non-edible products such as shoes and car seats found it nearly impossible. At one stage warnings were circulated around schools and offices about the presence of *haram* gelatine in ice creams, jellies and chocolates. With unprecedented speed, the government set up a body to analyse the problem and to everyone's relief most things were eventually cleared. Doubt was expressed, however, over certain french fries. The fat they were cooked in had been imported from the USA and had no halal certificate. This meant it could have come from cattle over which the correct prayer had not been uttered at the hour of death. The official statement detailing these discoveries also asked building contractors to avoid using certain paint brushes imported from China. They were, it explained, made from pigs' bristles and a house buyer's sensibilities, if Malay, ought to be taken into account.

One of the most difficult times for us as non-Muslims was during the fasting month of Puasa. It is compulsory at this time for all Muslims over the age of about 12, unless ill, to abstain from swallowing anything, whether food, drink, cigarette smoke or even saliva. Walking below the school balcony was a dangerous activity as pupils and teachers alike hoicked up their saliva and let fly over the edge oblivious of unsuspecting passers-by. Thoughts of sex, let alone the act itself, are also forbidden during the daytime. Sick people who cannot fast must make up the missed days later on in the year, on days of their own choosing, along with those women who were nursing or menstruating at the time.

We often thought of joining them in their daily fast for a few experimental days but, whether because of laziness in the face of having to get up at

5 a.m. or because of a lack of respect for involuntary acts of penance, we never did. Nevertheless, we could hardly eat and drink openly in front of the hungry and thirsty and although we continued to eat our lunch at the table in front of the kitchen window, we would lower the food from our mouths and stop the workings of our jaws to smile pleasantly if anyone passed by. Compulsory fasting often seemed pointless and unhealthy, especially when it posed an unwarranted hardship for pregnant women, sickly children and old people. Malay girls would faint at school assembly and when one child was seen nibbling in the school canteen the welfare teacher announced that the wrath of God would be brought down on her head. The admonition reduced the child to a blubbering misery.

When asked in the English lesson to write sentences about what they were afraid of, the Chinese and Indian pupils wrote of snakes and tigers while the Malays mentioned God. Islam is more than a disciplined religion. It is a religion based on fear and force, the fear of Allah's punishment for wrongdoers and a force derived from tremendous social and political pressure. All Malays, and indeed Muslims everywhere, must be seen to be fasting during Puasa. In Malaysia they are fined for a first offence and even imprisoned for recurring misdemeanours. Very few Malays will admit to illegal fast breaking. Perhaps the need to show a sense of Malay unity in the face of two diametrically opposite and threatening cultures, the Chinese and the Indian, prevents the Malays from readily admitting to the occasional illicit guzzle, although it is known to go on.

The period of fasting is thus one of solidarity. Malays everywhere gather together in the evening as the sun lowers towards the horizon, sharing the anticipation of their first food and drink for about 15 hours. The precise times for breaking the fast are published daily in the newspapers, accurate to the last minute and varying by up to ten minutes throughout the country according to the different angles of the sunset. For an hour or so before the appointed time, our neighbours congregated on the path outside their houses. Jokes and gossip were exchanged. There was more than the usual atmosphere of community. By 7.29 p.m. (or whatever the particular moment was) we could have walked naked through the kampong without being noticed by a soul. The traditional drum resounded from the local mosque, unheard and redundant in the age of digital watches and televisions. Malays everywhere were munching.

During the fasting month the long, daylight hours are to be endured with as little expenditure of energy as possible. School ended early during the month and our Malay pupils would flop across the tops of their desks with faint cries of "Puasa, teacher, Puasa." In contrast, the night was a time for liveliness. Those who intended to do little but sleep the following day stayed up all night eating and drinking. During the durian season, some would hold competitions, consuming as many as 20 of this enormously rich fruit in one night. Most people, however, awoke around 4.30 a.m. to eat and drink their fill before the fast officially began at about 5.30 a.m. in advance of even the first glimmer of dawn.

Towards the end of the month the atmosphere always started to take on a festive air. Fireworks became part of the evening celebrations and appeared to be lit with particular frequency about 3 a.m. Perhaps it was our imagination but it seemed that a disproportionate number of 'whistling moon flyers' were fired in the direction of the house of the sleeping infidels.

As Hari Raya, the great feast to end Puasa, approached, the people of the kampong would surround their houses with lights; simple oil lamps on the fence posts or electric fairy lights around the doors. The kampong looked very pretty and we were tempted to join in but we hadn't earned the privilege. We weren't Muslims and we hadn't fasted. Our house remained in darkness.

One evening, about a week before Hari Raya, we noticed a gathering of neighbours behind the house which had sprung up a few months previously beside our own. A van drove up and an enormous frying pan a yard in diameter was hauled out. Two of the women began pouring bags of flour into it and, as others added buckets of juice, the milk of coconuts, they both plunged in their hands and proceeded to mix it to a dough. That done, they lifted the pan over a freshly dug pit in which the men had built a fire and both settled down in chairs on either side to stir it in turns with great spades. Twenty-five pounds of sugar were subsequently added, five pounds of raw cane sugar giving the whole a dark-brown colour. The mixture began to thicken and bubble. The two stirrers gave up their chairs to another couple and so it went on, shifts of stirrers taking over from each other, constantly keeping the glutinous mass on the move, constantly guarding from sticking and burning. Darkness fell, the fast was broken in shifts and on they stirred, neighbours from all over the kampong gathering around the fire to chat and take turns with the spades. When we went to bed they were still busy and when Liam needed a feed at 2 a.m. they were still at it. A week later, at the Hari Raya celebrations, we were proudly presented with the fruits of their labour — a dark, thick, viscid and very sweet substance cut in rubbery squares which stuck to the fingers with the tenacity of glue and went by the name of *dodol*, a most important feature of Malay celebrations, a product as it is of harmonious and communal effort.

Hari Raya is the most important festival of the year for Malays. Its anticipation helps them through the long daily deprivations of Puasa, though as it approaches the hard work of cleaning the house and making cakes is made doubly arduous for the women. The actual date of Hari Raya is theoretically unknown. Before the festival can begin, as is the case a month previously for the commencement of Puasa, the new moon must be sighted. Astronomically, we were told by non-Malays, this is impossible on the first night and Hari Raya could confidently be predicted to start on the second night. This duly happened for our first Hari Raya in Malaysia. The following year, however, we returned from a short trip to the state of Pahang to join our neighbours in their celebrations. In Pahang the excitement had begun that morning but on arriving in the kampong we were astonished to find the inhabitants had broken the fast the day before. Vans with loudspeakers had disturbed their sleep to announce that the Sultan of Perak's religious advisors had sighted the moon and, contrary to other states, Hari Raya in Perak would begin a day early. We expected them to be pleased but they were most disgruntled. They felt their fast had not properly finished and to make matters worse, relatives arriving from other states, following their own states' rules, did not want to celebrate until the second day. Afterwards there were newspaper reports of people having been arrested for conducting prayers either a day too early or a day too late.

On our third Hari Raya we were intrigued to see what would happen. The Sultan of Perak this time announced in advance that he was to calculate the Hari Raya dates mathematically as is done in Saudi Arabia and settle the date for the first day. Conflicting stories and confusion continued, however, until the last moment. Then, suddenly, the King announced that the moon had indeed been sighted and the whole country celebrated together on the first day.

The feast itself generally consists of numerous dishes of tiny biscuits, cakes and jellies, often of a fluorescent hue and unbearable sweetness, which are constantly pressed upon the visitor together with drinks of strongly sugared water tinted with a red colouring beloved by Malaysians but carcinogenically suspect.

Our first Hari Raya was an education in Malaysian social behaviour. "Come at seven o'clock," we had been instructed by some neighbours who, being new to the kampong, had decided to put on a full meal of curries and rice in addition to the standard cakes. When we had failed to appear by 7.10 p.m. emissaries were sent to repeat the invitation. We trotted over, expecting an evening of chit-chat and food. On arrival, we were ushered to recently vacated places at the table and urged to "*makan, makan* (eat, eat)". Once finished, we gave up our seats to the most recent arrivals and joined the other guests who we noticed were all Chinese and Indian. The family's brand new colour television was on full volume. Everyone in the room was entranced by the antics of 'The Incredible Hulk'. Our few attempts at conversation fell on deaf ears. We too surrendered our attention to the box. At 8.30 p.m. the programme finished. Faces relaxed and we smiled politely around and eagerly began on pleasantries. *En masse*, the gathering rose and filtered through the chairs towards the door where our host and hostess stood, beaming, to receive the thanks of their departing guests. We lingered, and then decided it was time for us too to go. Car engines were starting up and others moved off down the kampong path. As we walked towards our house more cars drew up. We turned and saw our hosts, still at the door, greeting the newcomers. The new arrivals, this time fellow Malays, were shaking hands and moving into the house to begin their shift. We wondered which programme they would watch.

Hari Raya is, of course, a time for all the Malays to dress in their finest new clothes. This is one of the few times when the men can be seen in their national dress, a 'pyjama' suit, with a collarless shirt fastened up to the throat and at the wrists with tiny buttons. Over it is worn a beautiful silk, silver and gold thread cloth known as the *songket*, ideally woven in the states of Terengganu or Kelantan, and wrapped around the waist coming to just above the knees. On their heads they wear the traditional *songkoks*. The women, on the other hand, are rarely seen in anything but the *baju kurung*, an ankle-length skirt with matching long-sleeved top falling well over the hips.

Malay women are modest and never show their shoulders and rarely arms and legs in public. For some reason they never show signs of overheating in such garb either. When we arrived in Malaysia most of the women were bare-headed. Some, however, wore headscarves and occasionally we noticed groups of nun-like girls with their heads completely covered by veils of nylon drawn across their foreheads and tightly round their cheeks and chins, falling loosely over their shoulders to below bust level. We decided they must belong to a religious order. During our three years in Malaysia, however, we saw the fashion for *tudungs*, as they were called, spread. We watched dismayed as our Malay school girls progressed first into long skirts, then into headscarves and finally into *tudungs*. In schools where not a single veil was visible when we first arrived, they had sprouted like mushrooms. Particularly in rural areas the roads before and after school times were thronged with cycling girls, their turquoise skirts modestly covering their legs, their white veils fluttering in the breeze. Not a female head would be seen uncovered.

It was usually not the mothers who forced their daughters to cover up. Older women themselves were seldom seen in such attire, attractive embroidered white gauze scarves being loosely draped over their heads whenever they covered up at all. The influence instead seemed to come from the new teachers in schools. Young women fresh from training colleges appeared in greater and greater numbers in the *tudungs*. These younger teachers were often Islamic missionaries known by the name Dakwah who would hold religious classes after school for female pupils in order to disseminate Koranic teachings of which, to them, the covering up of all parts of the female body except the face and hands was an important aspect.

New recruits would then apply pressure within the family. Our next door neighbour's eldest daughter, at boarding school in Ipoh and heavily influenced by peers in her hostel as well as Dakwah teachers, telephoned home several times to find out if her younger sister was wearing the *tudung* yet. The latter had just entered Form One at the local secondary school and was thus considered to be of an age when boys might look at her sexually. Even previously uncovered female teachers, under pressure from colleagues and newly formulated State Education Department dress guidelines, began to appear in headscarves or full veil.

The *tudungs* were intended to hide the wearer's feminine charms. Strangely, the application of make-up did not appear to be in contradiction to this aim as the two were often worn together. Frequently high-heeled shoes with painted toe nails sticking out at the end could be seen trotting daintily beneath the long skirts. Most Muslims didn't seem to be clear as to whether exposed feet were permitted by the Koran or not. To be on the safe side, occasionally girls would be seen who had covered everything possible. Only the eyes could be seen and long gloves clothed the hands extending even to where the gap at the cuff might reveal an inch of flesh. It must have been intolerably hot. One trainee teacher who turned up for teaching practice dressed like this was actually sent away by the headmaster. The children, he pointed out, had great difficulty in hearing what she said.

At the University Science Malaysia in Penang the young Malay students had become so fanatical in their pursuit of modesty that they wanted the authorities to set down rules for all users of the new Olympic-sized pool, whether Malay or not. They recommended that all female swimmers be forced to cover down to their ankles and wrists and that all males should wear shorts reaching below the knees. Even for school sporting activities the girls' *tudungs* remained on their heads although they changed their *baju kurungs* for modest track suits.

It was not the fashion for the *tudungs* itself which we found so disturbing, but the fact that it seemed to represent a giant step backwards for the liberation of women and the mingling of the races. The girls wore with their *tudungs* an air of piety and unapproachability. They clung to groups separate from not only the boys but also the Chinese and Indian classmates with whom they had shared desks, jokes and homework only a year previously.

Our newly devout Muslim neighbour could not see that Malay Islamic fundamentalism led to the separation of the races. She taught her children to respect all people. Only in religion were they different, she asserted, and although Islam was resolute in its injunctions, it taught courtesy to non-Muslims. To our comment that Chinese and Indians felt the racial gap was widening, she said there was nothing to stop them from becoming Muslims! Islam was, after all, the "number one" religion in Malaysia. She then showed us a photo of her eldest daughter taken three or four years before in a mixed racial group, all the girls thoroughly enjoying themselves putting on poses and laughing, dressed only in shorts and T-shirts. She screwed up her face. It was shameful, she now thought, to see Malay girls dressed in this way just like westerners and almost indistinguishable from the Chinese and Indians. The Malays' new found dignity and self-awareness, she was certain, would make sure that it didn't happen anymore. As if to prove the point, juxtaposed in the family album were photos of the same daughter with groups of strait-laced Malay girls all fully wrapped in *tudungs*. In our neighbour's mind, as in the minds of most Malays, evidently there was no contradiction in encouraging a religious and thus physical distinctiveness from other races whilst denying that it led to ethnic separateness.

The Islamic revival of the last few years has therefore not missed Malaysia, and indeed partly because it is a multi-racial society with the Malays holding the political power in what they regard as their country, Islam and a forceful Islamic identity has become synonymous with Malay self-assertiveness. Religion has given the Malays, always economically inferior and out of place in prosperous Chinese Malaysian towns, a pride in themselves in a country with an inchoate national identity.

The extent to which Malaysia should become an Islamic society is the point at issue between the increasingly Iranian-influenced Malay opposition PAS and UMNO. PAS would like Malaysia turned into an Islamic state although they don't spell out how the economy would be run or what they would do with the Chinese and Indians if they did not willingly embrace Islam. UMNO as the leading government party has to be seen to be all things to all people. It mustn't worry the predominantly Chinese and foreign community that controls most of the Malaysian economy and it must satisfy the powerful Islamic tendency both in the party and the country at large, where the people have been carried along on the crucial question of Malay ethnic identity and its relationship to Islam.

To what extent UMNO government ministers and party leaders actually believe in the need to make television advertising Islamic or to have separate kitchens in hotels for halal and non-halal food, is a moot point. However, most Malay government ministers are sophisticated, often western-educated, men who invariably spend their holidays in European countries. It would seem that their neo-Islamic projects such as Bank Islam as well as the innumerable new mosques built recently are more than anything an appeasement to the strident militancy of PAS who accuse UMNO of being a party of infidels (*kafir*). By moving along the Islamic road, UMNO can forestall any attempt by PAS to win electoral seats in the Malay rural heartland on this highly emotive and potentially explosive issue.

5

Festivals and Funerals

The day was bright and sunny, but this was only to be expected. It never rained on the day of Thaipusam, our friend Sunraj asserted. Perhaps a few drops would fall in the evening as Lord Murugan's chariot returned to his mother's temple, but otherwise the devotees would be dry.

We had heard much about this festival which, although banned in India, takes place in many towns in Malaysia where there is a sizeable Indian population, usually around the beginning of February. The Batu Caves near Kuala Lumpur are the venue for the country's major celebrations but we had decided to avoid the notorious crowds there and go to Ipoh to watch the spectacle. Sunraj had offered to accompany us. An Indian of Tamil descent, he was perhaps our best Malaysian friend. He was a big-hearted, expansive fellow with a loud, explosive laugh and a generous white smile contrasting with his swarthy skin.

We had arrived in Ipoh the previous evening and had been lucky enough to see the procession of Lord Murugan's chariot. Lord Murugan, a brother of the elephant god, Ganesh, is the presiding god of the festival and a very important figure to all Malaysian Indians. A gilded and bejewelled statue of him resides in a temple in Ipoh which is dedicated to his mother Sakti. On the night before the festival it is placed with great ceremony and banks of flowers in a brightly decorated and lighted cart, known as the chariot, and pulled by two identical white oxen through the streets on a route to be followed next day by the devotees. Lord Murugan is then ensconced in a second temple, one which is actually dedicated to him, where he spends a night and a day before being returned to his mother 48 hours later.

As Lord Murugan approached his temporary resting place a wild-looking man, white dhoti flapping about his legs leapt into the chariot's path and with apparent fury hurled something at the ground below the oxen's feet. An explosion rang out and we jumped back. Water splashed our legs and more men ran forward with equal fervour. The impassive oxen plodded on, crunching their way over shards of broken coconuts. Lord Murugan had received a traditional act of homage.

Next morning we made our way to the river bank close to the temple where Lord Murugan was now in residence. It was a beautiful scene of exquisite calm. The river flowed smoothly and flocks of brightly saried women had collected in groups on the lush, grassy banks. Purples and yellows, scarlets and emeralds, brocades of gold and silver glowed in the light of the rising sun. Their hair decked with ropes of sweet-smelling white jasmine and their dark arms jingling with bangles, these women were dressed in their very best for one of the most important days in their religious calendar. A man sat in the middle of the nearest group wearing only yellow shorts, his intense expression echoed on the faces of his surrounding relatives.

"Weil-Weil, Weil-Weil," their chants began, Weil being another name for Lord Murugan. "Weil-Weil, Weil-Weil." His relatives concentrated their effort and collective will as they strove to help the devotee into trance. "Weil-Weil, Weil-Weil," they chanted in unison, a ring of sweating faces swaying back and forward around the blank-faced but grimly serious devotee, the sweet, soapy smoke from burning incense curling up around him.

Above on the bank, a group of white-clad musicians strained to encourage him. With drums and a type of long coronet they played furiously, a breathless, wild, racing cacophony which continued without ceasing as the chanting rose to a climax. The drumming quickened its beat as the devotee slipped into trance. One of the menfolk, appointed to take charge of the proceedings, pulled out the tongue of the now glassy-eyed devotee and dabbed it with grey ash. Then, as the drumming reached a tumultuous crescendo, the man raised a long silver needle and plunged it vertically through the tip of the devotee's tongue. We gasped with sympathetic pain but the devotee's face remained expressionless. There was no blood to be seen. He simply held his head forward so that another needle could be skewered horizontally through the sides of his mouth. Again no blood flowed and a little trident was attached to the point, linked by a thin chain to the flanged end. Preparations concluded, the devotee rose and calmly held up his arms to support a wooden frame, decorated with tinsel and peacock feathers, which was lowered on to his shoulders. Accompanied by his still-chanting relatives, he set off up the bank and across the road to the temple.

This frame is called a *kavadi*, but pronounced "*kawadi*" by the Tamils who, despite their rippling, burbling, tongue-twisting language, cannot for some reason manage the letter *v*. Devotees participating in Thaipusam usually carry them and even children bear small wooden ones. The devotees are those who have made vows (or "wows"!) and had their prayers answered. At the time of their vow they have undertaken to carry the *kavadi* perhaps once or perhaps for several years if their wish is granted, these wishes usually being for recovery from illness, to have a child or to find a wife. Those who have asked for a baby may even sling the child in a cradle from the bottom of the *kavadi*. For at least a week and ideally a month prior to the Thaipusam they must follow a strict vegetarian diet and abstain from sex. They must sleep only on the floor, not on a mattress and must not shave or cut their hair or nails.

We moved along the river bank to watch the other groups. The first devotee, we soon realised, had been an experienced one and as such could maintain a large degree of control. In one group a young man in deep trance broke through the surrounding cluster of relatives and despite their attempts to hold him plunged to the ground, leaped to his feet again and continued to convulse and lurch wildly as if possessed until the man in charge managed to restrain him. A woman from another group, overcome herself by the effect of the family chant, began to dance frenziedly, her eyes rolling, her folds of fat wobbling and was only brought to her senses when a handful of holy ash was smacked on to her forehead. She remained sitting, dazed, on the ground while the chanting group continued with the business in hand.

Urged by Sunraj we reluctantly left this amazing scene. The sun was by now strong, the river bank thronged with colour, the air filled with incense and the din of competing musicians. Our friend wanted us to see the "real *kavadis*". We made our way across the town to Lord Murugan's mother's temple. Only the less experienced or sickly devotees began their journey at the river bank, a few hundred yards from their destination. The majority crossed the town with their *kavadis*, a journey of a couple of miles.

When we arrived at Sakti's temple we found it jammed. In every nook and cranny chanting groups urged devotees into trance. The noise was deafening, the crowds almost impenetrable, the excitement feverish and the heat intense. Tongues were being skewered and additional needles inserted through the skin of the devotees' foreheads. Green limes, a symbol of purity, dangled from hooks which were being pierced through the skin of backs and chests. Like grotesque baubles, sometimes over a dozen at a time decorated the men's torsos. Outside the temple the devotees lifted on their *kavadis*. These were no simple wooden affairs but enormous metal frames up to twelve feet high and gaily decorated with paper streamers and tinsel, coloured balls and bunches of peacock feathers, the peacock being the vehicle of Lord Murugan. At night, Sunraj told us, the really big *kavadis* would come out, complete with coloured lights and portable generators! The weight of these structures was supported on the shoulders of the devotees. They must have been monstrously heavy but we were reassured that the devotee, once in a trance, possessed great strength and will power. Many *kavadis* were linked by chains to hooks in the back and chest of the carrier while others were attached by what resembled bicycle spokes, the whole thing looking like a gaily decorated instrument of torture.

One man had two parallel rows of hooks down his back which were fastened to lengths of cord. These reins were gathered in the hands of two young men, perhaps his sons. His skin bulged under the strain as he endeavoured to rush forward while they hauled on the cords to hold him back.

When the devotees had entered their state of trance and lifted their *kavadis* they moved out on to the street. Oblivious in their state of spiritual ecstasy some of them whirled and danced, scattering the accompanying relatives. The crowds gave an especially wide berth to two young men who emerged from the temple with spears, some ten feet in length, which had been impaled through their cheeks and, clenched in their teeth, swayed perilously on either side. A tall, striking holy man accompanied them, his long greying hair bundled high on top of his head, his forehead and arms streaked with patterns of ash, his beard brushing his bare chest, a crimson robe tucked around his waist. These boys seemed to feed off each other's trance. They would frequently turn to face one another and, their impassive eyes glued together, their spears in parallel formation, dance back and forth in slow circles.

At short intervals the groups set off, wending their way across the town to Murugan's temple. They were a strange sight indeed, the colourful *kavadis* swaying on the shoulders of near-naked, sweating, barefoot and entranced men, their impaled tongues protruding from their mouths. Alongside trotted the family parties, bright saris and white dhotis creating a pool of colour in the drab streets but almost totally disregarded by the passers-by, overtaken by cars and motorbikes, just another part of the traffic, the Indians doing their annual thing.

Towards Murugan's temple the crowds thickened. Along this part of the route makeshift stalls had been set up. These served to fulfil yet more vows as the owners dispensed free drinks to all who passed, whether devotees, followers or onlookers. These stalls were decorated with banana leaves and all had speakers blaring out distorted Indian pop and film music. The music from each stall clashed with its neighbours', the racing, optimistic cacophony adding to the already frenzied atmosphere. *Kavadis* streamed past. By now many of the followers, overcome by the atmosphere and the prolonged chanting, had succumbed spontaneously to the spell of the occasion and fallen into sympathetic trances. This seemed to affect particularly the women, their coconut-oiled hair straggling about their shoulders, their eyes wild, their normally demure, feminine poise abandoned as they danced, staggered and lurched along supported by less susceptible members of the family. Some sported needles on their lolling tongues having demanded them *en route.* Female devotees and even children did officially take part, but they could be distinguished by their yellow robes. Some of these women strode along, composed and purposeful, balancing metal pots topped with bunches of leaves on their heads in place of *kavadis*, a sign that they had made their vows to Murugan's mother Sakti.

On reaching Murugan's temple the devotees could not enter without first circling the building one, three or five times. A frenetic procession, they danced, staggered, plodded, whirled, strode, swayed, tottered and jogged the requisite laps. Some near the end of their strength were virtually dragged around the circuit while others at the height of their frenzy ran, their relatives struggling to keep up and restrain them from self-injury. Many, however, strolled calmly, their heads upheld, their dignity a result of profound faith and years of experience.

Once inside the temple they were relieved of their *kavadis* and swiftly subdued by a group of waiting temple officials. As one devotee followed another, they abruptly dabbed a handful of holy ash on their foreheads, rapidly removed needles, skewers, hooks and spears, smeared ash on the 'wounds' and turned them over to the care of their relatives. Most sank to the floor, exhausted, stunned and dazed to rest for a few moments and drink the coconut milk they had carried suspended from their *kavadis*, before heading quietly and submissively towards the altar to offer their prayers to the black stone figure of Lord Murugan.

The temple thronged with worshippers bearing plastic basins containing coconuts, betel leaves, bananas and incense. These were bought at stalls outside. An official at one side of the temple broke the coconut, discarding one half and the milk. The remaining half, with some squares of wax laid inside, was carried in the basin to the altar where a priest lit the wax from the holy flame. The flaming coconut was then returned to the owner who brought it home. Each worshipper also received a small handful of holy ash, prepared from burnt *padi* (rice) husk and applied to the forehead.

Beyond the immediate vicinity of the temple the air was festive. Stalls, set up all around, sold basins of coconuts, food and drinks. Families picnicked in the shade of the towering, sheer limestone cliffs against which the temple had been built. Girls trooped along the paths, their sleek hair garlanded with flowers, their slim, elegant figures adorned in their loveliest saris, the vivid colours all the more gorgeous for the contrast with their dark skins. They turned to gaze at us, the only white people present, and returned our greetings with dazzling white smiles and bright, flirtatious, giggling glances.

It had been an astonishing experience and we felt stunned and awed. The strength of these people's faith and devotion was overwhelming. We had seen flesh pierced before our eyes without apparent pain or blood. Moreover, doctors we asked said they had never once seen a case of sepsis resulting from these rituals, citing the piercing of limes with the needles prior to penetration as the possible explanation.

We had to be dragged off. Thaipusam was only the following year made a public holiday and we had to work that afternoon. It must have been a poor day's teaching. Our ears were ringing and our senses still reeling, our concentration scattered and our minds far from the mundane world of the past tense and guided compositions.

We had the chance in subsequent years to experience other Thaipusam celebrations in other parts of the country, but that first one in Ipoh remained for us the most impressive. The following year we happened to be in Penang at the time of Thaipusam. Perhaps we had drunk too much or stayed up too late at a party the previous night but we found the heat overpowering, the dense jostling crowds oppressive and the atmosphere altogether different. The crowd seemed dominated by young men clutching beer bottles and dancing frenetically in front of and around the devotees. Tight denim jeans outnumbered traditional white dhotis and drunkenness seemed to have the upper hand over religious trance, the devotees themselves seemingly inspired more by a self-centred pride in their macho feats than by religious devotion. In the thick crowds we were constantly on our guard against pickpockets and bottom pinchers.

One particular incident remained impressed in our memories. A tall man with somewhat menacing, sharp features had been overcome by the atmosphere. Evidently convinced he was a cobra he had pushed his way into one of the wayside shrines and had stationed himself before the altar, hands raised over his head in imitation of the cobra's hood, prancing, darting and hissing at anyone who came near. It was a fine imitation of this dangerous and much-feared snake and no one tried to oust him though the priest in charge was obviously not at all pleased with this intrusion. Perhaps the gods were seen to work in strange ways, for he was allowed to act out his possession unhindered until eventually he became tired and sank into a corner.

Just then we spotted a waiter friend of ours from Ipoh whom we hadn't seen for a long time. He had stammered as a child and had vowed to carry the *kavadi* for 19 successive years after he was cured. We had last met him just after his nineteenth Thaipusam, relieved that he had no more to do.

"What are you doing in Penang?" we asked, tapping him on the shoulder.

He looked round, surprise showing on his much thinner face.

"This year my b-brother is c-carrying a k-k-k-kawadi."

* * *

Our friend Sunraj, encouraged by our interest in Thaipusam, invited us to many more Hindu celebrations which he thought we would find interesting. These ranged from small family affairs to major celebrations in his town, such as marriages and, in one case, the sanctifying of a new temple. Once we went to see the emergence of a swami who had spent several days without food and drink meditating in a sealed underground pit.

We always felt warmly welcomed on these occasions.

"Come in, come in," a man urged us forward one evening as we hesitated at the threshold of the temple unsure whether to join the worshippers inside. "Welcome, do not be shy. Everyone is a Hindu."

We too were included in the prayers, we too had our foreheads stamped with vermilion dots and were passed the holy flame to receive its blessings. Once, while sightseeing, we noticed a collection of temple elders sitting on the floor lined up with banana leaves of food in front of them.

"Come, come," they cried when they spotted us, shuffling along to make room. "Come, eat, join us, eat."

It was perhaps easy in Malaysia to ignore the negative aspects of Hinduism since the caste system there, unlike in India, has lost much of its influence owing to the smallness and the mobility of the Malaysian Indian population.

Sunraj's family was very devout, in particular his mother, an aging, stooped, white-haired and often cantankerous old woman. A repository of religious wisdom, obligations, taboos and ceremonies, she ruled the roost with a firm hand and a hard eye, making sure the gods were accorded their due and never angered. In their living room a tiny shrine was renewed each evening with fresh water and a flaming lamp. Above, portraits of Mahatma Gandhi and President Kennedy looked benevolently down on the many occupants. In their garden another small shrine perched above the chicken coop and this too received its daily attentions. One side was supplied with a small curtain which was drawn to spare the sensibilities of the vegetarian gods inside if a chicken or goat was to be sacrificed.

Chickens and goats were ritually slaughtered for the great Indian Festival of Lights, Deepavali, to be served for family and visitors in spicy curries. According to Sunraj only married men could perform the sacrifice and one of his unmarried brothers had fallen ill for three days after doing so. When questioned as to the reason he turned to his mother and they burbled in Tamil for a few moments. Single men, he reported, are more likely to be sinful and thus displease the gods.

"Is your brother sinful?" we asked.

"Yes," he roared back, "he's a dirty crook!"

Whenever we went on trips around Malaysia we often found out later that Sunraj's mother had said a prayer for us, our safe return being attributed to her intercessions. When she had heard we were expecting a baby she had gone immediately to the temple to pray for its safety. Our son was two weeks old when we first took him to visit the family and, on Sunraj's suggestion, we made a trip to the temple.

The evening prayers were in progress when we arrived. The tall priest, his long, waving, oiled hair smoothed back from his face, strode purposefully around the temple, lighting lamps and bombarding statues with petals and holy water, chanting as he went. A few Indians stood around, men on the right, women on the left, their hands clasped respectfully before them. As the service ended the priest approached each worshipper in turn, an oval, metal oil lamp in his hand, waiting a moment for us to extend our palms over the flame and carry its blessing to our heads.

When the prayers were finished our friend approached the priest who agreed to perform a special ceremony for our baby.

"Lay him in front of the altar," Sunraj instructed us but we were loathe to leave our tiny, lightly-clad baby on the cold tiled floor. We knew he needed a feed and were afraid he would cry.

"He will not cry," Sunraj insisted. "I can guarantee it."

The priest had already begun his incantations so reluctantly we left him on the floor and joined our friend standing before the altar. Liam did not cry. Instead he turned his face, his forehead dotted with vermilion, to the altar and throughout the ceremony gazed towards it, happily waving his arms and legs. The priest busied himself before the statue of Ganesh. Chanting, he sprinkled the image with holy water, ash and petals, from time to time lifting the oil lamp with both hands, to encircle the figure with flame. Now and then the name "Liam" would catch our ears. The rest of his chant was a continuous, unpunctuated, litany of unintelligible Sanskrit. We asked Sunraj the meaning of the words but he couldn't understand the language either.

"He is simply giving the child his name," he answered.

Thus the ceremony proceeded. We moved from the central altar to first a niche on the right containing an image of the god Murugan and then to the left where a silver figure of Ganesh was ensconced. The same rituals were repeated before each, and all the time our little baby lay happily on the floor entranced by the lights.

Hinduism is one of the oldest existing world religions. It claims no single founder or prophet and no central concept of God. It is at least 3,000 years old and covers both primitive archaic beliefs as well as highly developed philosophical systems. It has a pantheon of countless gods most of whom, however, are actually reincarnations of the principal deities, Vishnu, Shiva and Brahma. In north India, Vishnu, the Preserver, and his various reincarnations are preferred but in Malaysia, where most of the Hindus are of south Indian extraction, Shiva, the Destroyer, features much more frequently along with his wife Sakti and his sons Ganesh and Murugan (Subramaniam). Ganesh's tubby elephant-headed figure can often be seen in Malaysian Hindu temples.

The average Hindu's life is filled with ceremonies. Engagements, weddings and deaths have their established rituals; there are also rites to mark the beginning of a girl's menstruations, stages of pregnancy, certain days following the birth of a baby, especially the naming at 16 days, as well as a girl's ear-piercing done at around the age of four or five.

We once witnessed the rituals celebrating the first menstruation of Sunraj's niece. Dressed in her best red sari, her hair, arms and neck hung with gold chains and ornaments, she sat enthroned in the best armchair, her feet surrounded by the paraphernalia of Hinduism — plates of bananas, coconuts, stainless steel water pots and oil lamps. Central to the proceedings was a huge flat rectangular stone and an enormous pestle, important implements in the Indian kitchen where they are used to grind chillies and other spices. After she had knelt at her parents' feet, the main part of the ceremony entailed all the girl's female relatives gently tapping her on both knees, both shoulders and the head, following a clockwise path, with first a lighted oil lamp and then flowers, a bag of rice and finally the pestle. Thus she was initiated into adult life, its sweetness and, for a girl, its endless domestic chores.

For many Indians these rituals are the very essence of their religion. By following them precisely, respecting taboos and attending the temple from time to time they feel reassured that the gods will look after their interests. The Sanskrit incantations of the priest have no meaning for them, the Hindu books of philosophy are rarely read but the gods are characterised by stories of their adventures, passed down from parents to children. There is, however, a real sense of belonging when the vermilion dot is pressed to the forehead and a sense of having received a blessing when the warmth of the lamp flame is wafted towards the face. To Hindus their religion may be largely incomprehensible but the exercise of its rites is a necessity for their peace of mind.

* * *

The Chinese in Malaysia follow a colourful and superstitious religion. Although they can claim membership of any one of three religions, Buddhism, Taoism and Confucianism, these three exist side by side and the Chinese tend to worship all simultaneously. Buddhism, imported into China in the first century AD, has taken on a particularly Chinese flavour and to some extent has been merged with the native Taoism and Confucianism. It would be all but unrecognisable to a Buddhist from the neighbouring country of Thailand where the form practised is distinguished by its emphasis on meditation and monasticism. In Malaysia temples may be dedicated to Buddha or to the Nine Emperor gods, to Kuan Yin the goddess of Mercy, or to any number of saints and deities, but most of them conform to a similar pattern. They are all ornately decorated, their curving tiled roofs being particularly intricate and colourful. Inside, gilt figures adorn the altar, frescoes and embroidered pictures cover the walls and dragons abound. Red is a favourite colour as it represents good luck and prosperity. The temple is invariably filled with the thick, scented smoke of joss sticks, clusters of which smoulder in large and prominent incense burners, implanted in the heaps of ash dropped by thousands of their predecessors. Chinese temples are the only places of worship in Malaysia (apart from churches) where shoes are kept on and as people are constantly scuffing in and out accompanied by the unhushed, strident tones of their various Chinese dialects, they are somewhat lacking in religious aura.

Some temples have particular attractions for which they are famous. In Ipoh a network of limestone caves is occupied by shrines and statues, the walls covered with elaborate and colourful frescoes depicting various oriental gods. Outside one is a pond filled with numerous turtles, symbols of longevity. In Penang a small temple is known for its numerous live vipers which entangle themselves around specially provided branches, lurk beneath tables and lounge on the altar. Motionless, they are harmless if left alone but potentially lethal if disturbed.

In addition to these temples most Chinese shops and houses have their own small shrines. Those at ground level are dedicated to the earth gods while the little red platforms fixed outside buildings at head height belong to the sky gods. These shrines are replenished, usually twice daily, with burning joss sticks and small cups of water and oil, the latter floating with a burning wick.

Confucianism exerts a strong influence even on the Chinese of today. More a philosophy promoting an authoritarian moral and social order based on family duties than a spiritual movement, it encouraged early traditional elements of ancestor-veneration to strengthen its impact. The result is a preoccupation among the Chinese with death and the well-being of the spirits of the dead. In consequence the emphasis on funerals is unrivalled by any other major religion. Unless placated it is believed that the dead person's spirit will return to plague the family so everything possible is done to ensure its comfort.

The spirit can enter any of the 14 levels of Hell or the seven levels of Paradise, according to the individual's sinfulness when on earth. Chanting by relatives during the funeral ceremonies, however, can build up a reserve of karma for the deceased and help him attain a higher level. Thus the longer the funeral, the more karma can be accumulated. Since customs differ according to the region from which they originated the details and emphasis of funeral rites vary depending on which linguistic group the family belongs to. However, the number of days involved must always be uneven, the longest funerals lasting for seven. The expense can be astronomical. A friend's father who died while we were in Malaysia had a five-day funeral costing the family M$56,000.

After being given a final 'meal', the rice being brushed across his mouth with a pair of chopsticks, the body of the deceased is laid out in an open wooden coffin, usually in the living room, with a photograph and a small shrine before it. The gathered family members are required to dress in black and for the duration of the funeral, many believe, must not bath. They are supposed to leave the house as little as possible and should not visit anyone as they are thought to be carriers of bad luck. Several times a day they assemble in prescribed order, with incense clasped between palms and in some cases sackcloth capes with peaked hoods over their black clothes, to follow the priests around the coffin, out to the street and back again chanting constantly as they go. These rituals, usually poorly understood by the participants, can last for an hour or longer each time as joss papers are burnt, cymbals clashed and karma accumulated.

Throughout the days of mourning the relatives are kept busy folding pieces of paper to create 'money'. Folded one way the paper is considered equal to M$1, while folded in a more complex fashion it is valued at M$50. Boxes of these papers, sometimes stowed in a paper 'safe', are burned at midnight before the day of the burial. It is believed by the Chinese that things destroyed in this way will re-materialise in the 'other world' as the property of the deceased and this belief has given rise to a flourishing papercraft industry. Shops specialising in paper belongings are a colourful sight. Not only money is 'sent up' in smoke but intricate paper houses with attached gardens, paper servants, flowers, palanquins and even paper dogs are burned. An average elaborately decorated house, some ten feet high, can take ten days to make and cost about M$300 but the expense can be much higher. Our friend's father was provided with a M$2,000 vineyard and in fact the paper artifacts alone accounted for a M$15,000 share of the funeral costs. To keep the old man amused in his new abode he was given a paper TV ('Hellevision'), a paper 'Hellevideo' and 'Hellecassettes' as well as a paper Mercedes to travel around in. In addition to the folded money, wads of high denomination 'Hell Bank Notes' are sold, printed (in English!) with the words "Currency for the Other World". All these things are burned in a huge bonfire along with the deceased's personal possessions – the mattress he died on, his shoes and his clothes, while a few intimate items, for example his spectacles and his comb, are placed in the coffin to be buried with him.

The following morning a feast is laid out on tables before the coffin, the food having been donated by relatives. Whole roast pigs, ducks and numerous other delicacies are put on display, the essence to be consumed by the spirit in the after-life, the rest to be eaten by the family after the burial.

The procession to the graveyard is a noisy one. Cymbals clash continuously to scare off evil spirits and relatives following the coffin set up a loud wailing. Pieces of paper are dropped along the route to act as a guide to the spirit should he wish to find his way home. One of our friends made the unfortunate mistake, while laying a paper trail for a Hash-house Harriers joggers' club race, of including a Chinese cemetery on the route. On the day of the race there happened to be a Chinese funeral in the town and several of the joggers ended up following the wrong trail – that of the funeral procession. It can only be imagined what confusion must have beset the poor wandering spirit!

The actual burial requires a great deal of attention. The grave must not be damp or under the shade of a tree so most graveyards are situated on hills. The direction which the grave faces is of utmost importance. A type of astrologer, known as the 'master of wind and water' is consulted to decide the precise compass point, basing his calculations on the age of the deceased, the number of his children and many other considerations. If the body is not correctly positioned it is believed to adversely affect the prosperity of the descendants for many years, even generations to come.

Once the funeral rites have been completed the deceased is by no means forgotten. Mourners must wear a little black and white rectangular badge on their sleeves for the duration of the period of mourning, usually at least 100 days. Close relatives are restricted in the colours they can wear. At first black and white only can be worn. Blue is then permitted, followed by the addition of green. Red, along with other bright colours, can only be worn when the official period of mourning has ceased. The time limit for each colour can vary from one month to one year according to the linguistic group involved. For a whole year after his death the deceased's place may continue to be set at the table and food served to nourish his spirit. On certain auspicious days of the Chinese calendar month more offerings are made to his spirit and more money may be burnt to keep him in funds. Many Chinese families take steps to ensure that all the offerings they burned at the funeral actually arrived. Mediums are engaged to make contact with the dead person, to ask if he is happy, if he is satisfied with what was provided and to ask if he has any further requests. As proof of his contact with the spirit concerned the medium usually provides the relatives with some information about the deceased which he would not be expected to know.

Throughout the year a number of Chinese festivals centre around the welfare of the spirits of the dead. On Ching Ming (or Cheng Beng) day families visit the cemeteries to clean up the graves, burn incense and offer food to their parents and ancestors. Pieces of paper are scattered over the grave. Later in the year comes the Festival of the Hungry Ghosts, a time when spirits of the dead are believed to return to earth and roam around in search of food. Great feasts are laid for them outside Chinese houses and although the food is eventually eaten by the familiy it is said to be lacking in flavour, the spirits having consumed the essence.

The Chinese have a reputation for being preoccupied with money. They have no qualms about praying for it in the temple, and are enthusiastic gamblers. They will work indefatigably and endure many deprivations to build up their businesses. Money is never far from their thoughts but perhaps this should be seen in the context of their beliefs. The more money they can provide for their funeral, the longer it will be and the more secure their spiritual existence after death. Conversely the more money a family can spend on the funerals of their nearest and dearest, the less likely he is to haunt them with misfortune after death.

The Chinese concern with funerals may also be held responsible for the large families they traditionally produced as well as for their liking for potency medicines and even for the frequent cases of female infanticide in days gone by. Only sons, and the more the better, can perform the funeral rites as married daughters join their husbands' families and switch their allegiances to his ancestors. In recent years, however, the trend is for smaller families as western ways of living catch on, and many of the religious rituals are being forgotten by the young. Many Chinese under the age of 30 or so are surprisingly ignorant of their traditional beliefs, never go to the temple and do not know the purpose of the household shrines. They do, however, participate in the elaborate funeral rites, often citing the sensitivities of the old people as their reason for doing so but perhaps the ingrained superstitions of generations will prove hard to discard and they too will eventually expect the same treatment.

* * *

Crackle, bang, clash. Multiple explosions rang out from the crowded street. A grotesque head appeared among the halted cars leaping, shaking and twisting towards us. Behind stretched its body, wending between the vehicles, bucking and rippling after the head. Led by a masked figure holding a fan the lion turned into the courtyard of the hotel. The manager solemnly lit a bunch of red firecrackers and the lion pranced, writhed and cavorted among the ear-splitting detonations, first in a circle then back on itself, undulating, advancing and retreating. The occasion was the Chinese New Year. Lion dancers bring good luck and prosperity to the houses and businesses they visit. They are rewarded with little red *ang pow* packets containing money. The manager had suspended some of these from the windows of the hotel. Among the exploding crackers the lion lifted its head and snapped the lower ones into its mouth. One more, with the largest amount of money, still hung, high up, well beyond the reach of the gaudy head. The lion was not to be outdone. The dancers perched on each others' shoulders beneath the long cloth body and the lion reared up erect. The dangling *ang pow* disappeared inside its jaws. Its work done, its reward received, the lion turned once more to the street and, prancing and swaying, headed towards the next customer.

The Chinese New Year falls in January or February, the date being dictated by the moon. It is the most important celebration of the year for the Chinese and the only one which closed down the commercial activities of our town completely. The market was empty and the shops shuttered. It was impossible to buy a newspaper or a loaf of bread. All the Chinese retreated to their houses and, dressed in their best, rested and entertained for two days. A multitude of superstitions apply to the Chinese New Year, varying, as with so many Chinese beliefs, according to the region of origin. They all, however, believe that to sweep the house on the first day will brush away the good luck for the year and will go to the extent of hiding the broom.

The New Year is ushered in, particularly by the Hokkiens, with the lighting of firecrackers. Even in our kampong, as midnight approached, we would hear the stuttering explosions from the town. It sounded as if machine-gun battles were being waged in the streets. Next day they were littered with scraps of red paper, the torn remnants of strings of fireworks, for in legendary times red — the colour of good luck and prosperity — had, combined with loud noise, driven away the *nien*, a ferocious animal with the head of a lion and the breath of a dragon, which had preyed on villagers in China every spring. Traditions die hard and this monster must still be kept at bay. Thus it is considered lucky for women and children to wear new red dresses for the New Year celebration and children must be given red *ang pow* packets filled with money to put in their pockets and keep them from harm. The house is decorated with red, and fruit on the family altar has red paper frills or squares attached.

About a week after the New Year celebrations we would be startled again, towards midnight, by the noise of bangers merging into a continuous, crackling hubbub. The large Hokkien population of the town was celebrating its escape from the Cantonese. In legendary times fighting had broken out between the two at the New Year and the Hokkiens, who were losing, had taken refuge in a sugar cane plantation. They were well hidden and after nine days the Cantonese gave up the search. Ever since, the Hokkiens have included a stem of sugar cane in all their festivities and celebrate the ninth day of the New Year with as much enthusiasm as the first.

The Moon Cake Festival falling in the eighth moon of the Chinese calendar is a quieter affair. According to legend, messages were secretly concealed in these cakes to aid distribution of plans for a national uprising at the time of the Manchu regime in China. The success of this venture is still celebrated. Cakes are, of course, made and eaten and at this time colourful stalls selling lanterns appear. The traditional lanterns are beautiful. Brightly coloured and painted cellophane paper is stretched over wire frameworks fashioned in the shapes of dragons, butterflies, goldfish, etc. Inside, a small holder is provided for a candle and the whole thing is suspended from a length of split bamboo. Children parade around the streets at night and take part in processions, these lanterns clutched in their hands, the colours glowing from the lights of the candles. In recent years more modern versions, made in Japan, have been gaining favour. These are lit by bulbs, turned on and off by switches on the handles and have more up-to-date shapes — Ultraman, spacerockets, Santa Claus and the like. Unfortunately many Chinese children now are too engrossed in watching the family video to bother with lantern processions. The lantern-making competitions which used to exercise their ingenuity are now largely a thing of the past.

It always struck us as sad that in a country of such varied, colourful, interesting and numerous festivals, each race pays so little attention to the ceremonies of the others. The Malays do not go near the flamboyant Chinese opera shows and the Chinese are indifferent to Islamic holidays. Frequently they give them the wrong names. Thaipusam is dismissed by the Malays as a pagan "weil-weil" event. The Indians generally ignore Chinese ceremonies. So three major world religions exist side by side in almost total isolation from each other, their festivities marked only by the extent to which they affect the commercial activities of the country at the time. The ignorance and lack of curiosity of each race for the others never ceased to appal us. So much potential mixing of the races is wasted, so much shared enjoyment is lost.

Paper Chinese funeral objects: a cardboard car with paper money on top and lucky joss papers below, to be burnt at the funeral to ensure comfort and wealth in the after-life.

6

Bomohs, Charms and Vampires

O ur huge neighbour shook convulsively with laughter.

"Why? But what for you want to see *bomoh*?"

"Because we're interested to see what happens. Because we're curious. That's why."

"Oh!" Bewildered, she gave up asking any more questions. Why would two *orang putih* school teachers, without a problem, want to visit a Malay medicine man?

"Could it be arranged?" we persisted.

A crossfire of rapid Malay among the other occupants of the room indicated that it could but we would have to invent a problem to tell the *bomoh*. This, we were reluctant to do.

Suddenly, the massive woman roared and banged her hands on her thighs so that the whole wooden house trembled from its effect. Then, when the tremor had died down, she stated categorically, "I have a problem."

She was the UMNO ladies' chief for the local area and it so happened that at the next election she was to be opposed by another woman. This displeased her greatly and she wanted some magic to influence the decision in her favour. We were shocked. Did she intend to stick pins in an effigy of her rival?

"No," she bellowed. "The *bomoh* use good magic." She wanted a *bomoh* to give her an aura, a charisma that all party members would see, thus realising that there was no alternative for the post of female leader but her: and with that she lifted her head, raised her nose and gave a downward curl of her mouth to make us feel that even before going to the *bomoh* she was a sure-fire winner.

The three of us set off in the afternoon, took a side road and found ourselves outside a traditional wooden house in an attractive Malay kampong. We stood at the low open doorway on the lintel of which a Koranic message was boldly inscribed. Inside, crosslegged on the floor, sat a wizened old man dressed only in a sarong and a green crocheted hat surrounded by the tools and paraphernalia of his profession. He was the local *bomoh, pawang* or traditional medicine man, a highly respected and influential member of the Malay community.

Two 'patients' were with him but he smiled and cordially invited us to come in. We took off our sandals, sat down on the floor and waited. The patients, an elderly Malay couple, were about to leave having received the 'prescription' for their ailments. Both were suffering from headaches and, having failed to get satisfaction from the local doctor, they were going home with some betel-nuts, neatly folded betel leaves and a white substance — powdered lime — all of which they were to chew with a little water. This would activate the salivary glands and the resultant red spittle was to be smeared over the head and around the ears.

The woman who gave us this information was meanwhile being

49

pummelled by our neighbour to the accompaniment of hoots and cackles. They were old friends. The elderly couple got up, collected their 'medicine', politely nodded in our direction and left. We tried to speak to the old *bomoh* but he just smiled benignly at us. His wife, also wearing a green crocheted beret, shouted that there was no point talking to him as he was extremely hard of hearing. How, therefore, was he going to advise our neighbour, we wondered. We didn't have long to think about it. Paper and pen were produced and she got down to writing the problems she wanted the *bomoh* to solve. It turned out she had another one concerning her husband's health as well as the leadership issue.

While she was painstakingly phrasing her points we looked around the room. Children and cats were roving in and out. A television was blaring out an English FA cup tie. It was a typical Malay living room with a glass-fronted sideboard full of plastic trophies. On top of it, imitation flowers and family photos lined up beside the Koranic homilies. On the walls garish western advertisements were stuck alongside more Arabic or Jawi words of wisdom.

The old man, having studied the first question, was about to begin. The *bomoh*'s home had conjured up an image for us, if not of a dingy incense-filled nook, at least of a place where there was a certain amount of peace and quiet. Maybe because this *bomoh* was partially deaf, the noise level didn't affect his concentration as he hunched over, mumbling incantations in a low, gravelly voice. He picked up a white cloth bag and took out two smallish iron implements, one a knife, the other a type of miniature axe head. These he tied cross ways with binding tape uttering "*assalamualaikum* (peace be with you)", an Arabic welcome. At a sign from the *bomoh* our neighbour heaved her enormous frame in front of him and notched her forefinger under the flange of the axe head. He placed his on the other side and started reading her first request. The implements were suspended by a finger each only. "*Ta tau* (don't know)," said the *bomoh* a moment later. Our neighbour looked crestfallen. We asked what had happened and she said that the knives had not given a positive indication as to the eventual UMNO winner. Apparently politics were beyond their scope.

The second request was handed to the old man, this time with a view to finding out what chest problem her husband was suffering from. Again the *bomoh* started muttering and addressed the tools with an Arabic greeting, and again the forefingers were wedged under the flange. He then read from her notes, slowing to enquire what the cause of the pain might be. He listed the number of possible conditions; heart attack – high blood pressure – diabetes – wind. . . . Suddenly the axe head twisted to the right. On the television Liverpool scored its second goal. The *bomoh* chuckled "angin (only wind)," pleased with himself.

"Ohhh," said our neighbour sounding convinced, but she didn't move.

The old man suggested they try again to make sure. This time we listened carefully as we watched. Heart attack — no movement; high blood pressure — no change; diabetes — nothing; wind — and the axe head swung to the right. "*Tentu* (definitely wind)," repeated the *bomoh* to the relief of our neighbour.

We learned later that this 'wind' was more than the simple flatulence that we had supposed it to be; rather it was a diffuse and ill-explained term used to refer to bad body humours. The *bomoh* wrote down the remedy — a bottle of water and three kampong chicken eggs. She was to go and get them and come back with her husband in the evening.

After sunset we all returned to the *bomoh*'s house, Mr Neighbour done up in a starched white shirt in contrast to the simple T-shirt worn by the 'doctor' *bomoh*. After the initial pleasantries were over, Mrs Neighbour produced water in a plastic container and three eggs from a bag. First of all she gave the container to the *bomoh* who, impervious to the surrounding hullaballoo, immersed a knife tip through the top. Then, holding the handle firmly, he lowered his head and recited a magical chant to bless the water. This over, he was handed the three eggs which he marked with a cross on both ends and strokes one, two, three on the centre of each. The first egg was held in both hands close to the *bomoh*'s chest where he welcomed it with "*assalamualaikum*" and an incantation. He then addressed Mrs Neighbour who, acting as mistress of ceremonies, ordered her husband to lift his shirt up to his neck. Intrigued we watched as the *bomoh* proceeded to roll the egg round his patient's chest. The egg was next pierced at the pointed end X, opened carefully and the white and bits of shell discarded. The yolk was carefully poured out on to a saucer and examined for portents.

"Look, two white bits," said the *bomoh*.

"Look, two white bits," repeated Mrs Neighbour conclusively to her lubberly husband. Mouth open he nodded agreement. He was then told to swallow the yolk and have a glass of holy water which he followed up with a terrific belch. "*Angin sahaja* (wind only)," said the *bomoh* and chortled contentedly at this literal demonstration. The other two eggs were to be swallowed on the following two days and washed down with the same consecrated water.

Mr Neighbour was also suffering from headaches. The axe head was consulted and the sun found to be the cause. His wife scolded him in rapid Malay with "I told you so". The treatment for this was a tiny onion which the *bomoh* took from his basket. It was halved and the flat sides laid on the back of his hand and flicked in the air. The half which fell round end up was discarded disdainfully with a sweep of the knife and the other half was used to make an X on Mr Neighbour's forehead, chest and back. Finally, the praying *bomoh* tied a knot in a length of black wool. Mrs Neighbour commanded her husband to expose his torso whereupon the *bomoh*, still praying, fastened the wool around Mr Neighbour's stomach.

This man was one of fifteen thousand *bomohs* estimated to be working in Malaysia today. It is a profession where the skills, as was the case with 'our' *bomoh*, are usually passed down from generation to generation. What we had witnessed, in spite of the Islamic cosmetics, properly belongs to Malaysia's pre-Muslim, Hindu, Buddhist and animist past. Malaysians of all races share a belief in the *bomoh* who, nowadays, can be Chinese or Thai, man or woman, as well as Malay. It is easy for Indian and particularly Chinese Malaysians to believe in the *bomoh*'s *jampi*, or magic, as their religions are so flexible. What seemed surprising to us was the apparent lack of contradiction for the Malays between *jampi* and Islam although it is possible that the *bomoh*'s 'prayers' are considered an esoteric interpretation of the Koran. The line between esoteric good magic and deviant sorcery or *seher*, something which all Muslims condemn as evil, often becomes a very tenuous and arbitrary one.

Charms meant to hurt people are definitely evil and against Islamic teachings. Other charms are harmless enough as when *bomohs* are employed for the Malaysian FA cup final to perform their magic on the pitch just before kick-off to keep away rain and ensure a dry evening's entertainment. Our neighbour's desire for mystical power over her political rival, however, could hardly be considered 'good' since it would have indirectly and unjustifiably harmed her opponent through diminishing her chances of victory.

Good magic should normally be used to cure illness and provide self-protection. After a series of mishaps to both Malay and non-Malay teachers alike at one of our schools, prayers were offered up by a Malay *bomoh* to help end the bad luck and invoke good fortune. As proof of their intra-communal efficacy, a Chinese man who had fallen off his motorbike a couple of weeks previously won, within a few days, M$800 on the 4-digit lottery. The Malays, for whom betting is *haram* didn't see anything wrong in accepting the fruits of his vice, the sticky drinks and sweet cakes which the Chinese teacher offered to everyone in celebration.

We thought Mr Neighbour had completed his unorthodox medical treatment when, the day after our visits to the *bomoh*, one of his daughters rushed over to tell us to come quickly. What a shock we got on entering their house! A man was sitting crosslegged on the floor with a cow-horn sticking out of the back of his head. An old *bomoh* dressed in a *songkok* was sitting on the settee.

"Come and see," welcomed Mrs Neighbour brandishing a coconut shell. "My husband do also," and with that she showed us a mixture of congealed blood and black hair lying inside the shell. "Look!" She indicated a couple of whitish specks in the coagulated mess. "This blood no good. Only bad blood come out, not good blood."

We learned that, although satisfied with the previous night's remedy for headaches, our neighbours had wanted to try another *bomoh*'s cure just to make doubly certain. A friend from the kampong had come along to have his headache relieved at the same time. This man was now about to have the cow horn removed from a shaved patch at the back of his head. We watched with mixed feelings of fascination and revulsion as the *bomoh* pierced a hole with a metal spike at the tip of the horn, breaking the force of suction and allowing it to fall away from the scalp. A largish lump of thick blood, which had gradually been drawn from nine small cuts in the skin, was scooped from the inside of the horn. The *bomoh* then re-applied it to the man's head, sucked furiously to extract more drops of blood and finally, taking one huge breath, covered the hole at the end with a kind of gum. The horn remained on the man's head until it was removed in the same manner about fifteen minutes later and the 'bad blood' taken out. Both men had two fifteen-minute sessions and were shaved and cut in exactly the same spots.

The 'treatment', apparently, can only be carried out after sleep, in the early morning or, when we saw it, late in the afternoon after a nap because it is only during sleep that the thick 'bad blood' is formed. The patient is advised not to go to bed too soon after the removal of the horn. The *bomoh* had been using this traditional method of curing headaches for 35 years with a high success rate, said the horn man, who professed to be feeling much better already. We asked if any magic had been involved and he replied that the *bomoh* had used *jampi* before shaving the head, making the cuts and applying the horn.

The Malaysian tendency to keep all options open had been first brought home to us when visiting a friend in a nearby town. He was an Indian and it was during the time of the Thaipusam festival when all the relatives near and distant had assembled for the great day. Our friend's house, which had been the collecting point, rapidly emptied as everyone took to the streets to watch the procession of devotees or dispense drinks and cakes to passers-by. For possibly the first time since the previous year not a soul remained at home. We joined the family for the festivities and eventually bade them farewell to return home. The following day on telephoning our friend to thank him for the previous day's hospitality we learned that, although the Thaipusam itself had ended successfully, there had been a family drama. Our friend's eldest sister had returned to the house to find all her expensive jewellery missing. A family meeting was held and the youngest brother offered to go into trance in front of the family shrine. This he achieved easily, talking in strange tongues to seek advice from the deities. When he had returned to a normal state he announced that the jewels had gone for a walk but would come back soon.

Not content with this verdict the old matriarch despatched three of her sons to three different *bomohs*, Malay, Chinese and Thai. The Chinese *bomoh* came to the house first and, muttering incantations, sprinkled salt all around the house and in the living room. Then came the Thai *bomoh* who cut cards and chanted. Lastly the Malay arrived and splashed some consecrated water around the house and in the living room. He then asked everyone present, all of whom had spent the night before Thaipusam in the house, to drink some of it.

All of the *bomohs* came to the same conclusion − the jewels had disappeared temporarily and would return. The cumulation of all this magic, particularly the drinking of water, was obviously too much for the culprit because the jewels were put back in their original place within half a day. The close family, it seems, had suspected one or maybe two distant relatives who the sister had thought were sleeping when she'd hidden the jewellery and this information had been communicated to the *bomohs*. No doubt the family believed in the insights from the youngest brother's trance and the power of the *bomohs*, but they were also aware, even in an oblique way, of the psychological impact on the thieves of the *bomohs*' presence.

Bomohs are sometimes, undesignedly, used in a role akin to that of western psychologists. A friend of ours had a brother-in-law, who was a shy younger son of fourteen in a very large family, and nobody paid him any attention. One day he became slightly crazed and started ranting. Our friend took him to the *bomoh*, who prescribed treatment with sanctified water and limes. The boy through the worry and active participation of members of his family in the rituals got all the attention he so obviously lacked and his 'condition' rapidly improved. From that time on, his parents became much more solicitous towards him. Elsewhere *bomohs* were regularly called into schools and factories to restore calm after outbreaks of hysteria, a frequently reported phenomenon usually attributed to angry spirits who had been displaced when the buildings were erected or to a jinx left over from the Japanese occupation. In some cases, the psychological boost from a *bomoh*'s attentions was enough to achieve cures where doctors had despaired and, in others, the overriding fear of a bad charm could render modern medicine ineffectual.

In general the first recourse was to medical attention. When a friend's sister, a woman in her forties, started suffering from fever and loss of appetite she was taken to the local hospital where she spent a month undergoing a series of tests. These failed to show what was wrong with her and after a further two weeks at considerable expense in a Kuala Lumpur specialist centre the cause of her illness was still a mystery. The family decided it was time for her to visit a *bomoh*. Fearing that she had been charmed, the sister did not want to return to her house but stayed with her mother at our friend's house, some 25 miles away.

One day soon afterwards we arrived unexpectedly at their home, in pouring rain, to find our friend was out. He later appeared, drenched, with a large bag of earth tied to the back of his motorbike, having gone on the *bomoh*'s instructions to his sister's house. We were astonished – fifty miles in the rain for a pile of soil; surely this was carrying things too far. But to him this was not a wasted trip. His sister had been suspicious of her neighbours for a long time. She and her family kept themselves to themselves and did not mix. It was possible, according to our friend, that, resentful of this, the neighbours had tried to bewitch her. In fact, he said, they had done it once before and she was fortunately able to dig around the house on the advice of a *bomoh* and find the bedevilling object, a bottle, before she became too ill. We watched as small bags of earth and limes were hung from the lintels of the doors and windows. Evil spirits do not like bitter things such as limes or onions and the earth presumably represented her home and thereby herself.

We left and our friend rang us up a few days later with the news that a miracle had happened. His sister was feeling much better, her temperature was down and her appetite was back. We were delighted and said we'd look forward to seeing him after the two-week school holiday which was about to begin. We didn't think any more about it until three weeks later when we met again.

"How are you?" we exclaimed warmly. "And how's your sister?"

His face dropped. "She's dead," he replied.

The reason for her death was never known.

If a Malay believes he has been or is likely to be charmed, he may wear a belt called an *azimat* with a special compartment inside containing Koranic verses to ward off the *jinn*. One was worn by a colleague of ours who, having won the heart of an engaged Malay girl, feared he might become the victim of an evil spell cast by her jilted ex-fiance as an act of revenge.

Although most *bomohs'* intentions were benign, occasionally in the press there would be reports of charlatans, one of whom claimed that all Muslims should follow him as he was a direct descendant of the Prophet Mohammed. These deviationist teachings were not tolerated by the government who immediately ordered the man's arrest. Others used their position to take advantage of gullible people, usually women, to swindle them or to have sex with them, saying it was essential to cure their 'disorder'. A favourite ruse of these disreputable characters was a 'magic' stone. Either the victim fell under its 'charm' and handed over his (or usually her) money or they paid up large amounts to possess it. One gullible young girl put one in her bath every day as instructed and only after her 'personal problem' had not been resolved within the prescribed number of days did she suspect she had been conned. A couple of women called on houses in our area selling face creams. When the victims applied some of the sample, they fell under the control of the women who promptly ordered them to hand over all their money and jewellery. One hapless woman who had no money in the house went so far as to withdraw all her savings from the bank to give it to the crooks.

Early on in our stay a friend, an assistant manager of a local rubber plantation, told us that there had been a number of *pukau* robberies recently in his estate. We asked what he meant and he replied that in *pukau* cases robbers were actually able to send house occupants to sleep or to induce a trance-like state using charms, herbs or incense.

"They just threw something through the window and the people couldn't move," he asserted. "Even the dogs went to sleep. Some of the people continued watching TV. The robbers just laughed at them and carted everything off, including the television."

We were anxious to know if we might expect a visit from *pukau* gangs.

"No," he immediately answered, "because you don't believe in it."

In another reported case, strange bangles with a peculiar odour were found in a drawer and blamed for the spell which stupefied the occupants of the house. These stories of *pukau* gangs were commonplace, Indonesian immigrants often being blamed with possessing the special powers and knowledge required. Sometimes *kemenyan* 'stones' (actually the fragrant resin benzoin), in varying combinations with poisonous fruits, seeds and even animal entrails, were said to be used to render victims insensible. To resist *pukau*, some *bomohs* suggested placing nails, red cloth and a fruit called candle-nut at strategic spots in the house, while others, perhaps influenced by Christian tradition or Dracula movies, believed a crossbar would prevent intruders from entering. One Haji (a man who has performed the pilgrimage to Mecca), counselled his fellow Malays to wake up and pray in the middle of the night to ensure a burglar-proof house.

The Malays on the west coast of Perak had a specialised method of stealing according to a Malay teacher friend and other people we subsequently asked. When Malays go to Mecca to fulfil the Haj (pilgrimage), some of them visit the local bazaar to buy a *toyol*, a kind of genie that can disappear and appear at the will of its master. The *toyol* sticks on the back of whoever buys it and follows his command only. It naturally becomes invisible when its owner meets people or goes through immigration (it doesn't have a passport!). Once back in Malaysia the Haji uses the *toyol* for malevolent purposes, usually to steal things from enemies. On the west coast coconut plantations, our friend informed us, Haji *toyol* owners are thick on the ground, all sending their evil genies to do mischief against each other.

"How do you know they exist?" we asked him one day. He said that *toyols* were sometimes careless and slow in becoming invisible. He knew people who had seen them, although he himself hadn't seen any. Once, in fact, his mother had turned round quickly when an unwelcome guest was present to see a *toyol* squatting on her shoulders grinning. It was a small, plump, gnome-like creature. It disappeared but by that time she realised her guest was up to no good and hid her money and jewellery.

Most Malaysians carry out some ritual before moving into a new house or even before building on the land to help protect them against evil. Our own house had been slept in for just one night prior to our arrival and to bless it beforehand, our Malay landlord ritually sprinkled water around the outside using a mango leaf as a scoop. Following this the juice of limes was squirted inside the house to cleanse it. Our neighbours had gone to the extent of putting old pieces of jewellery or money under their houses to protect them from misfortune and as a further safeguard, before entering the house, they would utter the word *"Bismillah* (in the name of God)." On a Thursday evening prior to the Islamic 'sabbath' this would be followed by a family Koran reading. In addition to the use of water and limes, Indians place smashed coconuts or leaves of the holy banyan tree under the foundations and eaves, while Chinese like to wedge pieces of lucky red paper between the bricks. Both Indians and Chinese also believe that an old coin hidden underneath the house is a powerful protection.

* * *

Tales of superstitious forces abound in Malaysia. One strange story we heard concerned a young Chinese rubber tapper who killed a king cobra snake when doing his rounds in an estate close to our house. As he delivered the fatal blow, according to his family, the cobra had looked up at him with human eyes. This event haunted him and when, two days later, he fell asleep in the same spot, he was discovered by his sister laughing to himself. He continued to behave strangely and a few days later did not return from his work. A search party found him dead in the pond where he had thrown the snake, his hands loosely tied and eight bricks in a plastic container around his neck. There were no signs of struggle or injury and the dead man had no enemies.

"King Cobra Case Takes New Twist," exclaimed a national newspaper the following day on its front page. According to the report, a policeman had had a dream in which the snake appeared before him and asked why the police had disturbed the place. No more was heard about this affair!

In Malaysia the 4-digit lottery is something of an institution and appeals particularly to the strong gambling streak in the Chinese. Once a week cars and motorbikes create traffic jams outside the lottery shops as punters drop by to check if their number has won them a fortune. The ticket buyer can choose his own number and the prize money is not divided between those who guess correctly; rather each winner can collect the fixed amount. If a popular number comes up the lottery shops stand to lose a lot of money. For this reason certain very popular numbers are banned. At the end of 1982 the number 1983 was disallowed but many betted instead on the number 1893. This proved lucky and the shops had to pay out considerable sums.

Punters choose their numbers from such straightforward sources as car registrations, birthdays, etc. but many treat their predictions almost as a science. The Chinese have a 4-digit lottery guide book which can be consulted like a dictionary as each word has a special number. Two children once closed themselves in a disused refrigerator and suffocated. The story was reported in the press and numerous punters picked up their books and betted. The number chosen, which was some combination of 'two', 'children', 'refrigerator' and 'death', proved to be a winner.

Punters will even go so far as to enlist the aid of the supernatural. Spirits, irrespective of race or religion, are regarded as helpful. Some friends of ours who managed one of the local petrol stations despaired of ever winning on the lottery. Then somebody advised them to enlist the services of a medium who, being in touch with the spirit world, would be able to tell them the next week's winning number. This seemed like a good idea and off three of them went to a *bomoh*/medium. This man said that in order to go into trance successfully, he would have to visit a place where there were many spirits. Therefore they all set off in a car to . . . a cemetery. The three men were feeling very nervous by this time but they resolved to go in. The medium, uttering incantations, then went into trance and producing a stake from his bag drove it into a nearby grave aiming for the heart of the corpse. Suddenly, the ghost of the dead man appeared before our panic-stricken friends.

"What did you do," we enquired open-mouthed.

"We ran off," replied one of them chortling. "We just ran off."

The medium, presumably, was left to discover the winning 4-digit number and return the dead man's ghost to its grave!

Four-digit number seekers never missed a chance. Once it was reported that a marble statue of the Buddha in the state of Johore was periodically emitting a reddish glow. This was hailed as a miracle and drew devotees from as far away as Penang. Village elders claimed it was a sign of good luck and prosperity for the local people but, when this was taken too literally, had to erect a sign requesting worshippers to refrain from asking the Buddha for 4-digit numbers. Another opportunity was seized when a giant yam plant started growing outside a woman's house in Penang. Although scientifically identified as a particularly large and rare flowering yam species, she took it to be a lucky omen and local punters came round in the hope that the plant might somehow give them a few 4-digit number tips.

* * *

Numerous ghosts and phantoms haunt the imaginations of the inhabitants of Malaysia, in particular the Malays. It was impossible to ascertain whether *orang minyak* (oily men) were human or fictional. These naked and reputedly handsome men molest unsuspecting women in their homes at night and if caught either slip out of their captors' hands or, according to some, turn into butterflies or rats.

In the history of the Malayan occult much has been made of the were-tiger. Aboriginal medicine men, seen as being on the fringes of the human and animal worlds, were supposed to be very skilled at changing into this greatly-feared beast. Nowadays, probably because there are so few tigers remaining, the field has been left untrammelled for the long-standing belief in vampires which are fortunately not dependent on a diminishing forest.

One day we noticed a photo in the newspaper of two small boys examining their toes. "Dracula Fear Grips Villagers," exclaimed the headline beneath. It was reported that a male vampire in the area had taken to sucking blood from small boys' big toes. Some children had even seen the fangs of the vampire. Police investigations showed that in the past the man's lust for blood had been "periodic" and that "only recently had the habit become serious."

In another report, four female factory workers, near Johore Bharu accused a fifth colleague, who was living with them, of sucking blood from their breasts. They evicted her and in the kampong to which she moved 'sightings' of the creature were reported. Some factory workers later saw her in a 'werewolf' state in a toilet. Women in the town were afraid to leave their homes but those venturesome punters had their priorities. Police had to plead with them to stop hanging about outside the house where the werewolf/vampire was supposed to be living, asking her for 4-digit numbers.

Another newspaper story from the same area reported that a woman had turned into a vampire after seeing a *bomoh* to make herself beautiful. She had been told not to look into the mirror for forty days following the treatment. However, she did so and, becoming ugly as a result of her impatience, covered herself up in the *tudung*. The *bomoh* then told her she could only regain her beauty if she tasted the blood of forty virgins. When seeking victims, she would greet them in a sing-song voice with "*assala-mualaikum*" ending with a repetition of the last syllable. Thus she came to be known as Kum Kum. A security guard in Kuala Lumpur claimed he saw the woman asking passers-by if there were any virgins in the area, but according to one version the warden of a girls' residential school had spread a rumour to find out which of her girls were not virgins. Since the Kum Kum woman was only seeking the blood of virgins, any girl who was not afraid, it followed, could not be one.

7
Marriages

We found the temple without difficulty. Strings of knotted banana leaves lined the entrance and two entire plants, complete with laden stalks of unripe fruit, flanked the gate. From the building itself came the unmistakable sound of an Indian wedding, the joyful, racing clamour of the *nathaswaram*, the long Indian coronet, and the tabla drums. Although it was eight o'clock in the morning, the astrologically auspicious time for this particular marriage, the temple was already crowded with resplendently saried women and white-robed men all chattering in Tamil. The floor was crowded with the paraphernalia of weddings; the saffroned, hairy coconuts, metal pots − one webbed with white threads − trays of red petals, yellow rice, bananas and vermilion paint, ornate, multi-wicked oil lamps and an incongruous plastic bottle of cooking oil with which to top them up. To the side of the altar stood the marriage throne, a double seat enclosed in a structure of mirrored designs and coloured lights, a small thoughtfully placed electric fan at the back. A priest busied himself energetically, the cord across his bare torso denoting his Brahman status, a plain white robe tucked around his paunchy midriff looking as if, at any minute, it might slip off.

Just then Chandran appeared. In his long, white, gold-fringed robes and ornate turban he looked a stunning figure. With a grave expression he followed his younger brother to the bridal throne, sat down in front of it and began the lengthy marriage rituals, sprinkling water and placing coloured powders, rice and petals as directed by the priest next to him. He had good reason to look grave. He was about to be married, largely against his will, to a woman he hardly knew, with whom he had nothing in common and who did not attract him. In his mid-thirties when we met him, Chandran was confused about his single status. Undoubtedly attracted by the idea of romance he was, however, a conservative soul and resisted any upheaval in his life. He lived contentedly with his mother. She washed his clothes and cooked food just as he liked it. She managed his money and tended him when he was ill. Like so many Indian men the bond with his mother was the closest he would ever form. What did he need a wife for? He had had a youthful passion for a very young Chinese girl. Her parents had been against the inter-communal romance but it still served Chandran well. When marriage was mentioned he sighed wistfully, indulged in a brief nostalgia, declared himself forever heartbroken and got back to tinkering contentedly beneath a car.

One by one his brothers were married. On each occasion the collected family took the opportunity to badger him. Why was he still single? They could find him a wife. His resistance provoked them. He was simply staying at home "enjoying" his mother, his eldest brother chided. Chandran became angry. He didn't like the accusation.

"Don't argue with me," replied the brother, incensed that one younger

61

than him should dare to speak back. "It was I who suckled first at our mother's breast."

Even a younger, but married, brother felt himself of sufficient status to add to the criticism. Chandran was rapidly losing face.

The family took over. Girls were sought. In a bid to retain control of the situation he acted on a last desperate romantic impulse. He had noticed a pretty young Indian girl waiting for a bus as he went to work each morning. He found out her name and telephone number. In a moment of rash impetuosity he rang her up and asked her to marry him. She put down the phone.

He resigned himself to the family's methods. The Indian population is relatively small in Malaysia and since unions within largely similar castes are more or less obligatory, the huge family network acts as a marriage bureau, putting out feelers all over the country. Names were mentioned, caste, status, looks and character discussed. Chandran stubbornly stipulated his conditions. She had to be "homely" (i.e. domesticated) and traditional. He did not want a "social" girl, one who wore T-shirts and jeans and had mixed too freely outside the home. Being somewhat scared of women he wanted one he could control. He also wanted her to speak English. He was proud of his own ability in English which in Malaysia is often synonymous with a good education.

A likely partner was found. Chandran seemed hopeful, even enthusiastic, after his exploratory trip to her house. The girl did not join in the afternoon party but made one brief appearance to serve the guests tea and cakes at which point her capabilities as a good home-maker were assessed. All this was done discreetly. Nobody actually stared at her as she came in but her carriage, clothes, hair and demure manner were all studied. She was found suitable and the union was agreed to, but when an astrologer was consulted their horoscopes did not match. Immediately the liaison was abandoned.

* * *

Chandran rose, the preliminary rites completed, and retired to the back of the temple. The music continued without ceasing, the horn player responding to the rhythm set by the tabla player as the two sat facing each other. The bride appeared. Stooped, as if in grief, she slowly made her way to the dais, supported on each side by consoling sisters, and proceeded to perform the same rituals as her fiance.

We wondered how she was feeling. Her face gave nothing away. She had expressed no emotion at the engagement either. Chandran's sister had found her in a small town about 70 miles from his home. After the family tea-party and viewing session at her house he had indicated his willingness to accept, being thoroughly tired of the whole business. At 29 she was considered a little old but their horoscopes matched and their castes were similar, hers being slightly below his. Chandran was resigned but, still dreaming of a true love marriage, he secretly arranged to meet her some weeks later. Perhaps one informal private meeting would be enough. For a week he was a bundle of nerves. He fretted over topics of conversation. We advised him to ask her about her hobbies.

"Well, what did you talk about?" we quizzed him some days after the meeting.

"Cars," he replied half-heartedly. "I didn't know what else to say."

Vijaya had listened carefully and replied "yes" and "no" to his questions. Her hobby was sewing.

"Didn't she ask you anything at all?" we enquired.

He reflected. "Oh, yes, she asked me if I loved her."

The engagement took place two months later. They had been seen together on their outing and when the news reached her family on the 'bamboo wireless' there could be no backing down. For Chandran, now, it was a question of honour. He had little to say on the subject of sewing and she had aroused no feelings of passion in him. He had taken on a duty.

The engagement took place at her home. The front of her father's shop had been cleared. Leaving a space for the ceremonies, the women were moving into position on the floor as we arrived, the single girls still slim and graceful, the older matrons hobbling about, pictures of care-worn corpulence, the products of too many children and too much oily, starchy food. Outside, the men relaxed on chairs. Chandran's presents for Vijaya were carried in from the car — a new sari, gold jewellery, cakes, flowers, bananas and coconuts. The first two items were borne away to adorn the bride, the remainder set down in the ceremonial area. The men from each family gathered for consultation. The discussion was formal but genial; we assumed they were making arrangements for the wedding. Just then a gold pendant appeared and the men examined it.

What we had witnessed, we later discovered, were the business negotiations, the financial arrangements. In Malaysian Indian marriages presents are usually given by both sides, by the man at the engagement and the woman's family at the time of the wedding. Vijaya's family, in this case, had been doubtful about the quality of the jewellery given. Chandran's family had felt insulted and his sister had responded with a remark about Vijaya's few white hairs. What had seemed to us an amiable gathering of simple Indian folk had in fact been an assembly of bitching and back-biting. Relations between the families did not improve. Chandran's family accused the other of low caste conduct. They had betrayed their "estate origins." The feud increased in intensity but arrangements for the marriage proceeded.

Now, however, the families thronged the temple together clad in their finest clothes. We were by now a little cynical of the picture of harmonious amicability which they presented, especially when we discovered that

Chandran's beloved mother, who had pushed him into this alliance in the first place, had refused to attend. The main part of the marriage was about to begin. Both partners, for the first time, took the stage together and sat side by side on the marriage throne. Relatives of each settled on the floor by the couple's feet giving each other vermilion *pottu* marks on the forehead and splashes of incense as a sign of good will. Without warning the music stopped and in the sudden silence the intonation of the priest could at last be heard. His words were solemnly chorused by those involved. Then, just as abruptly, the music began again, working to a tumultuous climax as Chandran slipped a cotton thread, bearing the gold *tali*, over his partner's head. The two were finally married. Guests jumped to their feet and hurled rice at them. Taking his sullen bride by the hand Chandran led her in a circle around the throne and the floor display of sacramental materials. Their circumambulations completed, the pair then exchanged their garlands of jasmine and sat again on their throne, edging as far apart as they could manage. It is customary for the bride, no matter how happy she is, to appear downcast, to keep her eyes to the ground as an expression of sorrow at leaving her parents' home. We wondered what Vijaya's true feelings were.

Suddenly a pretty, little girl of about five years old was carried forward, her face quivering with apprehension. She was plonked on to the knee of her uncle, seated before the throne and a sharp needle produced. According to tradition this little girl was to have her ears pierced at the feet of the bride and groom. Vijaya looked impassively on as the screaming girl, writhing with fear and pain, had her lobes forcibly punctured.

As the magnificent ceremony ended, family and friends queued to exchange the couple's garlands and offer them their best wishes. We joined them and from the bottom of our hearts we wished them happiness together.

When we saw them together for the first time after the wedding we were instantly relieved. Smiling, they waved to us from the window as we drove up. There was no sign of his mother.

"Vijaya, make some tea," Chandran ordered his wife. We were a little taken aback. This was a new forceful Chandran. Vijaya scampered off and we turned to our friend.

"Well, how are things?" we asked.

"Oh fine, just fine." He seemed genuinely cheerful. "Come and see my new room."

We had noticed a new partition blocking off a section of the main room. Inside were squashed a new double bed, wardrobe and dressing table. The couple had carved out a niche for themselves in the family home.

"All given by my wife's family," he informed us.

We returned to the living room. Vijaya appeared to set the sweet, milky tea before us. She offered us some cakes.

"Try one. My husband likes them very much." We were never to hear her call him by name. It would have been too disrespectful. With her hair tied in girlish bunches, freed from ceremonial restraints, she seemed much more lively. She chatted brightly.

We felt relieved. Perhaps our western attitudes had coloured our judgement. Chandran and Vijaya seemed quite content together, quite familiar. In the west our expectations are raised to unrealistic heights by films, advertising, fiction, etc. We constantly analyse relationships. We demand a lot of our partners and often our choice does not live up to our ideal. We regret our decision, look around at alternatives and the divorce rate soars. In Indian arranged marriages, however, the partners have not chosen each other much more than they can choose a parent or sibling and there is no room for regret. They generally make the best of it. Sometimes love grows between the partners, more often it is invested in the children.

We sat down to have a meal together. In the kitchen, on the other side of a flimsy partition Chandran's old mother was clattering around muttering to herself.

"Vijaya's food is rather saucy," Chandran commented. "I think I prefer it drier."

Shocked at this criticism we leapt to Vijaya's defence and declared ourselves very fond of saucy food. Our formerly modest friend was flaunting his new-found confidence, his new position as boss.

Chandran had a slight worry. He did not want to start a family yet. He wanted them to have a year to get acquainted first but, as they had been practically strangers at the time of the wedding, contraception had not been discussed. We promised to send them some booklets we had.

However, it was too late. When they came to visit us some weeks later it transpired that Vijaya had conceived almost as soon as the marriage was consummated.

After congratulating them we asked how his mother was. Chandran and Vijaya exchanged glances. They could have said nothing but Chandran was an open, truthful person.

"Well . . . ," he began, "but she is . . . What I mean is, actually, she and Vijaya are not getting along too well together."

It was obviously a sore point. Apparently the old woman had taken a dislike to her new daughter-in-law. Vijaya had made some remark about her to a relative and it had reached the mother's ears. She had not spoken to Chandran's wife for several weeks and had insisted that they cook separately, even going to the extent of hiding kitchen implements to make life difficult for her. Vijaya did not rage against her. She seemed to accept her lot quite stoically but, whether imagined or not, she came to feel that the family was conspiring against her. She had no job, she had little reason to leave the house and being a newcomer to the town she had no acquaintances there at all beyond her husband's family. When he went out to see his friends it was not her place to accompany him so she was left fretting at home with the uncommunicative old mother. She had relatives living several miles away but Chandran did not want to drive her there. In retaliation, when they made the occasional trip to her home town, she refused to visit his sister. On the surface the two seemed a reasonably harmonious couple. It was only Chandran's honesty which allowed us these insights into the actual dynamics of their relationship.

Time passed. It was hopeless for Vijaya to look for a post as a Tamil teacher, the job she had had before her marriage. Tamil teachers were not in demand, their hourly pay rates had been more than halved in recent months and no one wanted to take on an obviously pregnant woman. Vijaya waited patiently. There was a way out and she bided her time.

"My wife is returning to her home," Chandran announced one day. "She has reached the eighth month. It is time for her to be with her mother."

The heavily pregnant woman was bundled into the car and driven back to her home town. As is customary among Malaysians, and indeed Asians in general, the wife returns to her mother, sometimes a great distance away, who takes care of her before the birth and during the confinement period. There was to be another ceremony to ensure a safe delivery and we were invited to attend.

It was a disappointing affair. The house was packed with relatives but the majority were more interested in the video in the front room where they sat glued to a Tamil movie of romantic fantasy. A plump, doe-eyed girl, kidnapped by a couple of smarmy, moustachioed crooks, sang robustly as her prosperously-paunched lover raised hell and high water in his search for her. Meanwhile, in the kitchen, Vijaya, sweating in her heavy silk wedding sari, was perched on a stool. An old woman directed operations from the side lines. The rituals were performed, lamps waved, coconuts cracked and water splashed. We had seen this sort of thing once too often. It seemed like an elaborate excuse for neglect. The correct rites had been performed, the girl's well-being ensured, and the women joined the video audience.

A month later the baby was born – a girl. Chandran was delighted with his daughter. He travelled the 70 miles each weekend, eager to hold her in his arms. The confinement period passed. Some weeks later it was Deepavali, the Indian Festival of Lights. We were asked to make a trip again to visit our friends' baby. The family members were dressed in their best, crowded around yet another Tamil movie in the front room. We clucked over the baby who, though only two months old, had a great mass of curly hair.

"We plan to go to Penang next weekend. I made a vow in a temple there and we must bring the baby to have her head shaved. After that Vijaya will be returning home with me." Chandran was confident.

We were not so sure. She had earlier confided to us her intention to remain in her own home after the baby's birth. Later, as the four of us sat nibbling Deepavali delicacies at the kitchen table, Vijaya declared her intention to take up a job which had been offered to her locally, the following month. The atmosphere immediately became tense.

"But you are coming back with me next week," Chandran insisted.

Vijaya said nothing. Her eyes cast down, she sulked. It was not her place as a wife to challenge her husband's wishes. Her only option was to quietly disobey him when he was out of sight. Chandran had wanted a traditional, compliant wife but he should perhaps have chosen a younger woman. At 29 Vijaya had developed a will of her own.

"When you came home I did not mind if you stayed for a while, but now I want my daughter to be with me. I don't want to travel 70 miles each weekend to see her."

"It is your daughter you love, not me. You do not care to be with me."

It was true. Chandran could not reply to her accusation.

"In any case we need the money," she continued, seeing she had the upper hand. "Your salary is not enough. I must think of my daughter's future."

Chandran was stung. As a married man he expected to be obeyed. To his mind, he had satisfactorily established his position by bossing her around the house.

"A wife must follow her husband," he asserted lamely. That was the way of things. However, he was discovering that control was not quite as automatic as he had assumed.

Vijaya lowered her head and said nothing but it was obvious she was going to dig in her heels. The family was on her side. They had heard of Chandran's mother's attitude and, eager to resume the feud, had rebuked Chandran. Insults were traded once more and the young and inexperienced couple were torn between their deep affections for their families and their duties towards each other as spouses.

Chandran was accused of spending too much time with his relatives in the town rather than staying with his wife. Where was he on Deepavali Eve, she asked rhetorically. He had spent the night at his sister's house not with his wife. We couldn't blame him. It was obvious the family did not particularly welcome him and we guessed that Vijaya held him responsible for her long hours of pain on the delivery table. She had declared resolutely that she wanted no more children. Confused and unhappy, Chandran broke down and wept. The situation was impossible.

"She is like a dog barking at the moon," he complained. "She wants me to leave my mother, but I cannot afford to rent another house and support my mother as well."

We tried to find a solution for them. They had poured out their heartaches and grievances to us but our suggestions were inadequate. What experience had we in dealing with the burden of extended families; yet they needed their relatives. What did they have in common? How could they survive alone together in a suburban house? Theirs was a marriage arranged by families and those families were a necessary prop for it to continue. If Vijaya was to find work, a relative would be needed to look after the baby.

Chandran was forced to admit it was not fair for him to expect Vijaya to share his mother's house. Half-heartedly he promised to find a new place for them to live.

"But he will not leave his mother," Vijaya complained bitterly in private. "I know he will not."

She was right but somehow or other, when the baby was three months old, he persuaded her to come back. His mother had been brought to see the baby and a reconciliation had taken place.

"Better than I had expected, much much better," Chandran responded to our queries. He beamed. We had come to celebrate their first wedding anniversary. In his naively good-natured way he had convinced himself that his marital troubles were a thing of the past. His wife had returned to him. He cuddled his daughter to him. His old mother grinned toothlessly at us for the first time in a year. Vijaya sat on the floor beside the baby's bouncer. She smiled weakly.

"How are things going?" we asked solicitously.

"Oh fine," she answered without conviction.

Three weeks later she and the baby were back with her parents. She wanted to find a job, she said. She could not get one in her husband's town. Chandran was shocked. He felt she had made a fool of him. Far from being a smug, masterful husband it was obvious to all that he could not "control" his wife.

"This time I am just going to let her be," he told us. "She must make up her own mind."

Within a couple of weeks, to our surprise, she was back with her husband. Only later did we discover the reason. While with her parents she had missed a period. Within three months of the birth of her daughter, during her brief return to her husband's bed, she had become pregnant once more. Her fate was sealed. Her family made it clear to her that her place was with her husband. With one young baby and another on the way, she was in no position to opt for independence. This time there was to be no more running away. She settled down, even got a temporary job and the two began talking of buying a house of their own. They had a family now. They were forced to accept their responsibilities. They had a foundation for their marriage.

* * *

With Vijaya and Chandran there had been no dowry in the traditional sense. They are Tamils whose grandparents came to Malaysia from south India and since the majority of south-Indian Tamils were originally poor estate workers who could not afford dowries, the system largely died out. The Malaysian Tamils of Ceylonese descent, however, came to Malaya mostly to work in white collar, administrative jobs and regard themselves even today as a cut above the Indian Tamils. In order to preserve their separate identity and status they have retained the dowry system intact. A Ceylonese woman who marries an Indian man will generally forfeit her dowry. A Ceylonese man who marries an Indian woman will be held in contempt in the Malaysian Ceylonese community.

A 33-year-old Ceylonese acquaintance of ours went to Malacca to 'view' a girl whose parents offered a dowry of M$100,000 for his hand.

Asked the beautiful 20-year-old when he was introduced to her, "Do you love me?"

He, having met her for the first time one minute before, said, "Of course I do."

She — "But will you love me for ever?"

He — "Definitely."

On returning home, the man changed his mind. The parents rushed to see him. The bidding went as high as M$200,000. A car was offered, a house . . . but our acquaintance had decided that he loved somebody else.

Dowry, when given, should theoretically provide some wealth for the daughter in her own right. According to our Malaysian Ceylonese Tamil friends, the bridegroom should ideally be 30 to 35 years old, experienced in the ways of the world and financially secure, having established himself in some capacity. (Our acquaintance was a rather shadowy businessman.) The girl should be between 18 and 24 years of age and totally inexperienced in life and love. If she's over 25 or so, the chances are she may know too much and possibly even have had contacts with other men, whereas if she's just a 'young seedling', the man can take her and plant her and let her grow according to his design. Like the faithful dog she will have total allegiance to him. There will thus be much less chance of her disobeying him or being unfaithful to him. He, in turn, must look after her as one does a little sister. Low, indeed, would be his stock were he not to protect her from leering men or cosset her as far as possible in a cocoon of financial security.

* * *

We had in Chandran and Vijaya's case had a rare insight into the workings of an Asian marriage. The relationships between other couples were largely closed books to us. Those which we observed among the Malays of the kampong around us seemed harmonious enough. The women did the housework and the men were the bosses. Sticking to their traditional roles there was little reason for conflict. In any case they are, by and large, a reserved people not given to displays of temper who avoid discord as much as possible.

In addition the men are unusually home-loving, spending much of their free time playing with their children.

Indian-style arranged marriages between complete strangers are rare among the Malays, but the families play an important role in organising the matches and often the bride and groom are not well acquainted even though their union may be termed a love marriage. Not many children marry against their parents' wishes although what happened to one of our neighbours would be unlikely to happen nowadays. Her parents had married her, at the age of 18, to a man 13 years older. A boy her age had wanted to marry her but she had accepted her parents' guidance. The course of their 18-year marriage had been far from smooth.

"You *so* happy," she would accuse us frequently. "My husband go to Ipoh." Her lip would curl with disdain. She suspected he had a girl in the town.

On one occasion we told her about our friend's wedding. The girl, an Australian whom she knew, had married a Malaysian. We didn't specify his race.

"Is he Malay?" she eventually asked as this vital information, despite her promptings, was obviously not forthcoming.

"No, Indian," we replied.

Her face assumed a look of anguish. "But why . . . ?" Her tone was tragic — such a nice girl, but what a fate!

"Because they love each other," we replied.

"Oh!!!" she exploded, laughing. "Love!"

Poor woman. At 36 she had borne all her children, achieved gargantuan bodily proportions, lived half her life in a passionless marriage and had an uninspiring yet unfaithful husband. Nevertheless, deep in her heart she longed for romance.

* * *

Every school holiday we would be invited to two or three Malay teachers' weddings. Beforehand, as the date approached, adolescent-type jokes would be made in the school staff room as the Malay men anticipated the pleasures of married life. Married Malay women frequently took some part in these jokes but the unmarried ones always pretended that they didn't know what was going on.

We had scarcely arrived in Malaysia when we were invited by our landlord to a relative's wedding. Both teachers, they were getting married at the end of the long holidays. We arrived to find a festive atmosphere in the street where it was to be held. Wooden posts and zinc roofing had been erected, blocking traffic but allowing people to eat the curry and rice and drink the crimson-coloured beverage without being either roasted alive or soaked to the skin, depending on the caprices of the weather. We felt a little awkward. We were new enough to the country to expect someone to come and talk to us but instead our plates were heaped with rice and curry and our glasses constantly topped up with the lurid sweet juice to the accompaniment of the twin exhortations "*Makan* (eat)" and "*minum* (drink)".

At last, when we felt our mouths blistering and our teeth decaying we were bidden by the bride's mother to enter the house. In a corner, two tall, wooden chairs sat throne-like on a dais. We stepped through the sea of seated women and were shown into the bridal chamber. A huge double bed, the one on which the newly-weds were to spend their first night, was covered in gold-embroidered cushions, lace netting draping the sides. A side fan was prominently placed next to the bed to ensure a cool night's nuptial bliss. We were then shown to a room where all manner of very sweet cakes were aesthetically arrayed on the floor awaiting the couple's attentions.

"Would you like to see the bride?" we were asked. We nodded and were escorted to the back of the house. We imagined her, willowy, virginal and tremulous, a young, shy, gentle maiden. The door opened. An enormous, spotty woman coated with thick, badly-applied make-up, her lacquered hair stuck with gaudy, gilt ornaments, confronted us with a wide, lip-sticked grin. She took our present and returned hurriedly to work miracles in front of the mirror.

As we returned to the living room there were murmurs from a few loosely-veiled old women sitting near the door. The groom and his retinue had arrived. A slight, stern-faced young man dressed in *songkok, baju melayu* and *songket*, was ushered past the playing children into the room to the uncoordinated thumping of the *kompang* drums. He sat down on one of the wooden chairs staring mournfully in front of him. Seconds later the bride appeared clad in a large gold-embroidered, crimson *baju kurung*, and eased herself into the other seat. Without looking at her husband she gazed dolefully at the ground.

This was the *bersanding*, the principal part of the Malay marriage and is originally a borrowing from the similar Hindu ceremony. They had been married legally by the kadi (religious judge) quite some time beforehand but the customary laws prevented them from living together until the traditional festivities were over. As they sat in state, King and Queen for the day, crowds of well-wishers gathered round to admire them and to take pictures. Then the oldest women, followed by other female relatives and friends, ascended the makeshift dais to bless the bride. She received the touch of their hands with her hennaed palms closed downwards on her *baju kurung*, her eyes averted.

This completed, everyone concerned themselves with watching the piercing of some girls' ears, leaving the 'Royal Couple' immobile on their thrones sullenly examining the mats in front of them. Eventually, at a sign from one of the older women that time was up, the bride and her husband were led to the repast. Interest in the proceedings was rekindled as they positioned themselves for the preliminary nuptial spread.

After the conjugal night together, the bridegroom would return to the state of Kedah where he had been posted as a teacher. They would then see each other possibly once or twice on long weekends before the first term holidays. This is a common state of affairs for many Malays who, working as government servants, can be arbitrarily posted around the country. Many newly-marrieds, especially teachers, spend their first year or so working at opposite ends of the country until, their new status taken into account, one of them, usually the woman, is given a transfer.

Traditionally easier for Muslims, divorce is commoner among Malays than other races. Indeed the fear of being rejected and left to fend for themselves is one which haunts most married Malay women. Every morning one of our neighbours would warn her husband, as he left for work, not to flirt on the job, threatening to rush straight to his school and create a scene if she heard of any misbehaviour. This man's father had had three wives and his grandfather twelve! Like father, like son, she feared, and kept a sharp eye on him. Many women in the kampong had husbands working in distant towns and the likelihood, in such circumstances, of the men finding second or alternative wives was obviously greater. Until recently the man could quite legally remarry and maintain up to three more households without even his first wife's knowledge. Now, however, the law has been changed and she must give her written permission. Also divorce has been made much more difficult to obtain than in the old days when the words "I divorce you" needed only to be repeated three times by the husband for it to become a reality. Now there must be grounds and an obligatory period of attempted reconciliation.

The position of divorced women is the same no matter what community they come from. They are considered to be the party at fault and are unlikely to get married again although the men bear no such stigma and can easily attract another bride. The women are generally left with the children to care for, perhaps with no financial assistance. In 1982 civil marriage was made compulsory for all non-Muslims. (Muslims are registered by the religious kadis.) This was to put an end to the abuses caused by customary marriages which could be declared null and void on whim and gave the wives no legal rights at all. The Chinese, in particular, frequently married second and third wives without needing to divorce their previous ones. Very often, in the old days, having left one wife in China, they would remarry in Malaysia while still sending money back to the first wife. The owner of our local sundry shop returned to China in early 1984. Having come to Malaysia at the age of 21, leaving a wife and two sons in his home village, he had remarried and fathered twelve more children. Now at the age of 72 and with his second wife dead, he was at last going back to his native land and to the wife he had left 50 years previously.

Celibacy has no place in Islam. The only answer a single person can give to the Malay question "*sudah kahwin?*" – "are you married?" is "*belum*" – "not yet." For anyone, especially a woman, to choose to remain single bewilders the average Malaysian. Only in some places such as Kuala Lumpur and Penang are a few westernised women rejecting what is socially expected of them and even then they are often anxious and confused about their status. The Chinese believe a person who dies single will enter the children's department in hell and to avoid this an unmarried person may be ritually married to a paper figure at his funeral. In fact the greatest pressure to marry is perhaps on the Chinese, partly because a large family means more help with the business and partly because of traditional Confucianist beliefs which require male offspring to maintain ancestor worship.

Chinese men and women have more freedom to mix than Indians and Malays, and much more frequently choose their own spouses. In cases where it is necessary, however, a match-maker may be employed and will receive a fee if the marriage takes place. The ceremony bears little resemblance to the Indian and Malay weddings. Preliminaries require the bride and groom, in their separate homes, to dress completely in white for a ritual hair-combing, welcoming them to adulthood. For the actual wedding, brides nowadays often wear a western bridal gown instead of the traditional red high-necked *cheong-sam* but there are no other Christian overtones. The couple bow briefly before the household shrine. Then the most important ceremony, the serving of tea by both the bride and the groom to their own and to each other's families, takes place. It is only after this that they are considered to be properly married.

One thing the marriages of all races have in common is the complete dominance of the man over the woman. She will wash all his clothes, cook his meals and clean the house. A man who helps in the kitchen must, it is believed, be under the control of his wife, and no self-respecting husband will be seen there. Even if the woman holds a full-time job and brings in half the income she is expected to perform all the household chores without his help. The burden of tradition is so heavy, moreover, both on women and men, that there is little impetus for change. The women accept their subordinate role; the men see no advantage for themselves in sharing work and play equally with their mates.

* * *

We ourselves got married in Malaysia in a spontaneous ceremony which managed to incorporate elements of the marriage traditions of all the three main races. The morning began with a quiet, relaxed civil ceremony at the local registry office where we took the necessary vows and signed the appropriate papers. The real wedding, however, took place that evening in Ipoh at the house of our good friends, Jan (Australian) and Chong Peng (Chinese Malaysian).

We arrived to find lengths of sugar cane tied to the door posts of their stilted wooden house and signifying, according to Chinese customs, that a wedding was taking place inside. We headed towards the kitchen intending to help with the preparations for the party but instead a bottle of wine and two glasses were thrust into our hands and we were instructed to go upstairs to the bridal suite and keep out of the way.

In the evening we emerged to discover the open area beneath the house transformed with bunches of orchids and ropes of sweet-smelling jasmine criss-crossing the ceiling. Two chairs had been placed throne-like on a dais with a cloth backdrop, as for the Malay *bersanding*, and when guests had finally arrived we were ushered into them.

Our friend Sunraj stepped forward with two garlands of jasmine and as he slipped them over our heads the assembled company pelted us with yellow saffron rice. Following Indian traditions we stood up and exchanged our garlands and then friends filed up one by one to exchange them for us, wishing us happiness as they did so.

The ceremony was not finished. Sunraj stepped back and Chong Peng appeared with a bamboo basket which he set at our feet. Baffled, we looked closer and a pair of chickens blinked warily back at us. Then, with a grin, Chong Peng laid more offerings on top of the basket. There were red eggs representing fertility, noodles to symbolize longevity and two little sweet cakes to bring us sweet happiness. Finally he handed us a pair of scrolls, each of which unrolled to display a four-foot length of red and gold paper neatly painted with a series of black Chinese characters. One, according to Chong Peng, read "male and female phoenixes together in intimate love"; the other, "everlasting happiness, like mind and heart and a very auspicious union."

"But the chickens?" we queried when he had explained the other gifts to us.

"They act as a guide for the bride to her husband's home," he answered. "They are yours to take home and look after."

We hadn't bargained for such responsibilities quite so early in our marriage. But we were left with little time to consider the matter. Champagne was produced and eastern traditions gave way to western celebrations. A wedding cake iced with clusters of frangipani flowers appeared and when the toasts were finished Scottish dancing began.

It was very late when the last guests departed and we tottered back upstairs to the bridal chamber. The air was scented with ripe mangoes from the tree outside and the full moon beamed down through the coconut palm fronds. A slight cool breeze stirred the mosquito net which enveloped our bed in a fairy-tale cocoon. We could not, we agreed, have had a more special wedding, nor a more magical place to have had it.

No one stirred early the next morning. The sun rose, the brief coolness fled and the chickens in their little bamboo basket began to feel desperately hungry. By the time we got up, to our great consternation, they had wriggled free and run off. Fortunately they reappeared, but only to die in mysterious circumstances, in the care of our neighbours, while we were away on our honeymoon.

Superstitious friends feared for the success of our marriage but they needn't have concerned themselves. The accumulated good luck from following so many traditions stood us in good stead and the various fertility rites included in them were quick-acting indeed. The seeds for a happy marriage had been sown.

8

Orang Asli

During our stay in Malaysia we were frequently reminded that there were three races in the country: Malay, Chinese and Indian. This is, in fact, untrue but it is perhaps a measure of how little impact the small Orang Asli population makes on the lives of most Malaysians, not to mention the economy.

One day, while driving to the Cameron Highlands hill station, we suddenly spotted a wizened old man striding along the side of the road clad merely in a loincloth, a blowpipe in his hand. We looked more closely at others we passed and realised that, although more conventionally dressed in torn T-shirts and shorts or sarongs, they were not Malays, as we had assumed, but Malaysian aborigines. From time to time we caught glimpses of their villages of attap huts positioned close to, but below, the road, almost entirely hidden from sight. We were curious. We wanted to stop but were unwilling to intrude, so instead continued on our way, part of the procession of cars filled with lowland dwellers seeking a weekend in the cool temperatures of the hills.

A few months later in Taman Negara, the National Park, we had a closer encounter. Bird-watching in the tropical rainforest is a neck-breaking experience and we had discovered that the most comfortable method of observing birds which frequent the upper canopy of the immensely tall trees was to lie down flat on our backs on the paths. We were so engrossed in observing a flock of green broadbills that we did not notice the approach of a group of four Orang Asli hunters. We eventually sat up and lowered our binoculars to find them smiling bemusedly at our extraordinary behaviour. Without a word they then filed past us, their tough, splayed, bare feet moving noiselessly on the forest floor, their blowpipes over their shoulders, dart quivers hanging at their waists.

This was one of the few encounters we ever had with "nature's gentlemen"; the Orang Asli Negritos. Of the three 'waves' of Orang Asli immigration into the peninsula they constituted the first and now inhabit the most geographically isolated areas — the dense interior forests of the northern half of the peninsula. Although their origins are unclear it is thought they came from the Andaman islands about 10,000 years ago. Numbering around 2,000, physically they are the most distinctive of the Orang Asli categories being short and dark with Negroid features and frizzy hair. Traditionally they lead a nomadic life-style, gathering roots and fruits, and killing birds and small animals such as squirrels and the occasional monkey with darts from blowpipes. Larger animals like deer and wild pig are caught in traps or snares, all game, irrespective of who catches it, being shared among the members of the group. (It seems that in the 1950s the Negritos were understandably bewildered when the communist insurgents tried to instruct them in the egalitarian ideology of Marxist-Leninism!)

It is quite difficult to come into contact with these nomadic people

77

who are on the whole very shy and will, if they hear someone approaching in the forest, step into the bushes to avoid contact. Some, however, have accepted jobs as guides for people who want to climb the largest mountain in Peninsular Malaysia, Gunung Tahan, or who simply want to experience life in the rainforest. The men make excellent guides with their unique knowledge of forest paths, sources of food and water and their intimacy with the wildlife.

This involvement with the outside world has led to drastic changes in their lifestyle which particularly affect their families. We occasionally saw groups of women and children close to the National Park headquarters, squatting under palm attap lean-tos, typical of their temporary forest dwellings, and leading unnaturally sedentary lifestyles while waiting for their menfolk to return from expeditions. The area had quickly become exhausted of the roots and tubers which the women traditionally collect so, using the men's wages, they were buying food from the National Park store. The encampment quickly became littered since these forest dwellers had not yet learned to distinguish between a discarded leaf and a tin can. While it can be said that the Negritos have never been very careful about standards of cleanliness, neither have they needed to be, since they would always move on to another clearing after two or three days when the surrounding food supply was exhausted.

The Orang Asli we had seen along the Cameron Highlands road were not Negritos but belonged to the Semai tribe, one of several which comprise the larger Senoi ethnic category. The Senoi are considered to have been the second major influx of Orang Asli who arrived in the peninsula, probably about 6–8,000 years ago. Now numbering about 35,000 they are found in the central mountains of Malaysia in the states of Perak, Pahang and Selangor. They speak a language related to that of the Mon-Khmer people which is different from the Negrito dialects, although the latter contain many Senoi words.

Our opportunity to meet these people came when a teacher friend mentioned that, as an active member of the Baha'i religion, he fairly regularly visited a few of the villages where the inhabitants had joined his faith. Being the most accessible of the Orang Asli, many of them along this road have, over the last forty years or so, been converted to the Christian, Baha'i and, to a lesser extent, Islamic religions from their own animist beliefs in the spirits of trees, rocks, etc.

Leaving the road we slithered our way down the soft, muddy slope, clinging to each other for support, running and skidding the last couple of yards to the first of the stilted attap huts. Children scampered sure-footedly behind us. Small yellow dogs which had growled timorously at our approach retreated to a safe distance, cowed by admonitions from the inhabitants of the hut who peered at us from the doorway with placid, mildly curious expressions. The response to our Baha'i friend's greeting of "*Abor*" had been friendly but not exuberant. Shy people, the Orang Asli are inclined to retreat from contact with outsiders. They had watched our undignified descent into their village with interest but their welcome for our friend despite his long association with them was reserved.

We climbed up a few steps into the house and, slipping off our shoes, treaded our way carefully across the creaking floor of split bamboo to where the best mat was being laid out for us to sit on. We had entered the house on the uphill side where the door was fairly close to the ground. However, on the downhill side, where we now sat, there was a drop of about 10 feet between the floor and the ground. Apart from a two-foot-high bamboo barrier, presumably intended to prevent small children from falling out, the rest of this side of the house was completely open to a magnificent view. Beyond the four or five other huts of the village, the hillside dropped away into the valley and then rose steeply again on the other side clothed with an unbroken mantle of primary rainforest. Far below a crested serpent eagle circled above the invisible river. Directly underneath us chickens, dogs and a few goats foraged, waiting to consume any scraps of food and waste pushed through the gaps in the bamboo floor. A couple of impish boys shinned easily up and down the long stilts supporting the house.

Several women sat inside the hut, one nursing a small baby. Like the men, on the whole they seemed smaller than Malays and had broader faces with more prominent cheek bones and wavier hair. Intermarriage between Semai and Negritos, however, makes it difficult to talk of pure racial types. On seeing us enter the hut the woman of the house stirred up the embers of the fire and pushed a couple of tapioca tubers into it. In every Orang Asli house a fire is kept constantly burning on a specially constructed platform in the middle of the floor. Her husband, his mouth stained with the red juice of the betel-nut, was busily occupied putting the finishing touches to a long rattan fishing rod. He would use it to catch fish from the river in the valley or from the nearby National Electricity Board dam. The fish, however, were small, he told us, and much less plentiful than in former times, a possible result of increased pesticide use in the Cameron Highlands.

When the tapioca was cooked, it was passed around. Fibrous and starchy it reminded us of both roasted potatoes and roasted chestnuts, but the extremely dry consistency was less than appetising. Unlike hill rice, which is difficult to cultivate and is considered by them to be a rich man's crop, tapioca grows in practically any kind of soil and it is the staple food of nearly all settled Orang Asli. Indeed from what we saw and heard on this and subsequent trips to the Semai settlements, the people almost totally subsist on a diet of this tuber, nibbling at it constantly throughout the day.

The Senoi, unlike the nomadic Negritos, are traditionally shifting cultivators, slashing and burning patches of forest to clear fields and moving on to new areas only when the soil becomes exhausted. These people, however, had been settled in this spot for several years and did not plan to move. Some of the men told us they worked from time to time as grass cutters at the National Electricity Board station or as casual labourers on the Chinese vegetable farms in the Cameron Highlands. Most of them did not wish to be tied down to a routine job which goes against their traditional way of life. Working on the vegetable farms usually meant staying there for two or three days at a time and for their efforts they received M$10 daily plus a few vegetables too old or too small to be sold. Those who were lucky enough to own a few durian trees could make a good profit in the season. Earnings were not subject to the same rules of sharing as food, and any money gained by an individual was kept by him.

We had just been served with tea, presented in the best plastic mugs on a battered but prized tin tray, when a young man entered the hut and greeted our friend. He had just returned from a three-day trip into the forest to gather rattan. Sold to Chinese middlemen this creeper is a valuable source of income and, cleaned of its thorny outer casing, can fetch M$2 per foot length. Strong, yet flexible, it is used extensively in Malaysia for furniture making.

These Orang Asli also collect bamboo from the forest selling most of it for 60 cents per 20 foot lengths. It is also indispensable to the Semai themselves: their houses are made of it and lengths of bamboo held in place by forked sticks connect their villages to the source of water. Looking around the room, we noticed baskets and utensils made from bamboo tucked away in cross beams along with blowpipes and quivers, fishing tackle and dried bunches of maize which would be planted around the settlement in the drier months as a variation from the diet of tapioca. We asked to see a blowpipe and an old man shuffled over to show us. It was about seven feet long and made from a single piece of bamboo. The quiver contained numerous small darts, each about a foot long and smeared at the point with a kind of dried red-black paste. The old man was adamant that we should not touch them because the paste, the sap of the poisonous Ipoh tree, is deadly, remaining effective for up to a year after it is concocted. The poison kills the prey almost immediately but does not affect the edibility of the meat except in a small area around the wound, which is immediately cut off after the animal dies.

The women, by now used to our presence, began to ask us questions. They seemed to be somewhat more outgoing than the men and one in particular puffed vigorously on a wad of coarse tobacco which she had stuffed into a cone of leaves. The rattan collector chatted to our friend as he nibbled at a freshly baked tapioca root. His face was downcast and it transpired that three of his four children had died that year. Although official statistics show a drop in infant mortality in recent years, belief in the powers of the *bomoh* and distance from government clinics means that all too frequently children still die unnecessarily.

A lot of children we saw were suffering from skin diseases which were at least partly due to poor nutrition. Because they no longer practise shifting cultivation and because there are fewer fish and forest animals to provide vital protein, their diet has worsened. The soil around the settlements is not now fertile enough for anything more demanding than tapioca and maize since land in the tropics, once cleared, is quickly denuded of its fertility unless replenished with fertilisers. Some of the Orang Asli have also, through contact with the wage economy, become lazy about cultivating. Gardens far away from the settlement have often been abandoned and the little money that is earned does not seem to be spent on nutritious food items.

Living on the edge of two types of civilisation, these people are not apparently benefitting much from their contact with mainstream society and are fast losing the skills and knowledge of the traditional lifestyle which has maintained them for so long. Education, although available, is showing no signs of helping the younger generation to bridge the gap. The children are most reluctant to live in a hostel 20 miles from their village in order to attend a secondary school where they believe other races look down on them. Furthermore the parents see no reason to encourage them.

It was time for us to leave. Afternoon was turning to evening and our friend had been told of a new settlement nearby which he wished to visit. With cries of "*Abor*" all around we clambered up the slope again to our car. Suddenly we felt embarrassed at the clutter of consumer goods displayed to view, a reminder of the great gulf which lay between us.

The new settlement was only a few miles up the road. The four or five huts were much cruder than those of the village we had just left — low bamboo platforms on stilts sheltered by hastily constructed lean-to screens of attap. Most of the inhabitants were content to gaze at us from their perches in these huts but one young man, well-built with strong, muscular legs and tousled, long hair jumped down to speak to us. An elderly couple, hunched and emaciated, emerged from their hut, standing close by to survey us inquisitively but most of the children remained near to their parents, staring passively at the intruders.

We had at first assumed that these people must still be practising the traditional shifting cultivation of the Semai and that they had moved to this spot in search of new land. The decision to create a new settlement, however, had been taken because of illness and death in their previous village. It is still common to burn a house after a death in it and this is probably now the only reason for leaving an area and setting up a home elsewhere. Destroying the house frightens the spirit and by moving elsewhere they can leave it behind. Spirits of the dead are greatly feared by the Semai and burial grounds are always situated on the other side of a river from the village since the spirits, they believe, find it difficult to cross water.

We were both shocked by the wholesale felling of trees all around the settlement. We felt it would make more sense to have kept them for shade and to prevent wet mud from pouring down the steep hillside every time it rained. The Semai, however, will never put their dwellings near or under trees because of the danger of them collapsing during thunderstorms of which they have an extraordinary fear and which they believe are a punishment sent by the spirits of ancestral deities for sinning on earth.

As we talked we noticed, lying on one of the platforms, a pile of strawberry-shaped fruits with thin, dry shells. On seeing our interest the man offered us one to taste. The white flesh inside was juicy and bitter but not unpleasant and we were told that they came from the root of a common plant which grew all around the camp.

The sun was sinking. On the way home our friend reminisced about his early days in the state of Negri Sembilan where he was brought up. One of his favourite haunts, he told us, had been Tasek Bera, a huge, reedy lake bordering the state of Pahang, where numerous Orang Asli resided in villages scattered around its shores. Although he had only been able to reach it by motorcycle he had heard that a new road had been built and urged us to visit the area. On looking at a map we discovered the lake to be fairly close to a scientific research centre and forest reserve we had been planning to visit and decided immediately to extend our trip.

It was only when we were halfway to the lake that we realised why the atrociously pot-holed road along which we were crashing, banging and crunching, to the peril of our exhaust pipe, had been built. After miles of freshly planted oil palm and rubber estates we suddenly crested a hill to find a landscape so devastated that we gasped in horror. Only the burnt boles of the larger trees remained as evidence that not long ago this land had been covered with virgin rainforest. Otherwise the landscape, reaching almost as far as the eye could see, was completely bare, blackened by fire and devoid of life. Far in the distance some forest still stood but as we drove towards it lorries, loaded high with gigantic trunks, approached and passed us, grinding their way slowly along the rutted timber track. In what remained of the forest, when we finally reached it, the loggers were hard at work and the whirr of the chain-saws was a stark reminder that it wouldn't be long until this patch of forest too was reduced to ashes and sad stumps of once-majestic trees.

Eventually we arrived at Fort Iskandar to find no more than a couple of corrugated iron shacks, erected originally by the British in the '50s at the time of the communist insurgency known as the Emergency. It was then that the administration first became more than peripherally concerned with the aboriginal population. Being apolitical and friendly people they had either willingly helped the insurgents, as they had aided the anti-Japanese forces during the occupation, or had supplied them with food and shelter under the threat of force. Several of these forts had thus been built throughout the remoter areas of the peninsula as army posts to enable a closer watch to be kept on the forest people. To cut the communists' supply lines, thousands of Chinese squatters on the jungle fringes were forced to move into specially constructed New Villages where many of them still live. A similar solution was suggested for the Orang Asli and in some areas communities were forced to move to the vicinity of the forts. This experiment was not successful. Crowded together, the Orang Asli soon used up local food supplies and disease spread swiftly throughout the encampments. Forced by this, and the depressed morale of the people, the authorities had little option but to let them return to their homes.

We stopped our car outside the main building, a type of run down hostel, and hesitantly approached the door not sure how we should explain our presence there. A group of young Malay men called us in and offered us seats and tea. Several were sitting around an untidy table finishing a crude meal of rice and tinned fish while others lounged in rattan easy chairs. On one table a few maps and charts lay flapping in the breeze. The men, it turned out, were surveyors, employed by the Central Pahang Development Authority to draw up plans for an Orang Asli reserve in the area. It had been decided that since so many of them were being displaced by the clearing of the forest a special tract of land should be declared inviolate and preserved for them.

We enquired about renting a boat to visit the Orang Asli settlements around the lake but were told there was no point since most of the people had moved closer to Fort Iskander, into the area of the proposed reserve and we could easily visit them in their village only ten minutes away by foot. "*Sana, sana*," — "over there," the surveyors directed us, flapping their hands in the air. It was obvious that they had no interest in the village at all and were extremely bored and disgruntled at having been posted to this remotest of places.

Misdirected, we ended up at the lakeside. While we were admiring a collection of one-man wooden dug-out canoes tied up among the reeds, an old man appeared carrying planks of wood which he placed in one of them. He was in the process of moving his house to the village reserve and his tale of woe was one echoed by many more Orang Asli when we finally reached them.

On entering the village our first thought was that we had again taken a wrong turning and ended up in a Malay kampong. The neat, stilted houses, hung with potted plants were identical to so many we had seen elsewhere and the people who peered at us looked remarkably similar to our neighbours. It was only when we noticed the timorous pie dogs, typical of

Orang Asli settlements and shunned by the Malays as *haram*, that we realised we were in the right place.

The people of this area are of the Semelai tribe, belonging to the larger category of Proto-Malays, who came to the peninsula about 4,000 years ago and are considered to be the earliest precursors of the Malays. Numbering about 25,000 and living mainly in the southern states, these are the Orang Asli who have integrated most with the Malays, the majority speaking standard Malay (the Semelai mixing it with Senoi languages), having Malay names and following a Malay lifestyle without, however, being Muslims or considering themselves Malays. (One exception is the tribe of 2,000 or so *Orang Laut* — Sea People — living in the state of Johore who have been Muslims for centuries.)

Once we had taken the initiative and begun speaking to one man others approached and most of the afternoon was spent chatting as we squatted outside one of the houses. The men were glad to talk and told us without prompting of how their traditional means of livelihood had been taken away from them with the destruction of the forest. We found their openness surprising and refreshing after the more subdued Semai people. Until recently the area had been covered with thick lowland forest which had provided them with roots and fruits to eat and sell, wood for their houses and boats, animals for food and rattan to sell and make into things. Now, with the forest gone, they had been forced to become wage-labourers being paid the customary M$10 a day to perform menial tasks on the new plantations. When asked about the motorbikes which buzzed through the village giving to it an air of prosperity they pointed out that these were essential if there was to be any income in the community as the young men had to travel long distances to their work before dawn each morning.

With regard to alternative sources of food, the lake itself had few fish and marauding elephants herded together in the remaining patches of forest destroyed any crops that the Semelai tried to grow. Some Semelai families did own one or two acres of rubber trees the latex from which they sold to Chinese middlemen in return for essentials. The Semelai, as with other Orang Asli, sometimes become financially indebted to the Chinese although the ones we met did not express any bitterness towards them.

Their tragedy is the tragedy of a people who shared but never really owned the land, who had hereditary rights to hunt in, collect fruits from or cultivate a piece of land rather than to possess it. They only received compensation for the loss of productive land where rice or cultivated fruit trees were grown. For the loss of hereditary forest they received nothing.

We asked one of the Malay reserve planners if the Orang Asli were forced into these reserves. He said that the *batin* or headman was persuaded by the government to move into them and the villagers followed him. All the Semelai we spoke to, in spite of their ready smiles, were very unhappy about their present and future situation. The Malay had argued that medical health care was much better and easier to organise when the Orang Asli were grouped together in reserve land but he overlooked the fact that this grouping can also lead to despair when the people are separated from their traditional way of life.

With this experience fresh in our minds we decided to visit the Department of Orang Asli Affairs in Kuala Lumpur. The Deputy Director was suspicious of our desire to find out about the workings of his department and defensive about the government's policies with regard to the Orang Asli. He said that whatever mistakes the government has made in the implementation of its policies, its good intentions to improve the position of the Orang Asli should not be questioned. This we did not doubt although an Orang Asli to whom we later spoke and who had worked in the department said that there was a great deal more talk than action. A report on the Orang Asli written by the Deputy Director seemed to back this up. Of the M$40 million allocated to the Orang Asli Department under the 4th Malaysia Plan (1981-5), the great bulk had been spent on the burgeoning department itself including salaries, equipment and the maintenance of existing services. Development expenditure for schools, machinery, plant seedlings, hospitals, etc., which was less than a third of the total, had in fact been reduced from the figure of two years previously.

In its desire to bring about a united nation state with inhabitants of approximately the same living standard — a commendable notion — the department has decided that the Orang Asli need to be 'guided' towards development and integration. 'Non-development', i.e. remaining nomad or practising shifting cultivation, would be more harmful to the Orang Asli, in their opinion, than what they call properly planned 'directed change'.

To this end the department has implemented a 15-year regroupment programme which began in 1979 with five 'package' type schemes where each Orang Asli family, which has been displaced from its traditional land, is given ten acres of rubber/palm oil or fruit orchards, a dwelling with two acres for maize, rice or tapioca, access to a school and hostel, medical facilities, a cooperative, a hall, roads and community land or forest. In addition, by 1978, 12,000 acres for hundreds of smaller schemes, each 50 to 100 acres, had been set up for the development of the Orang Asli, supervised by Field Officers. This certainly looks good on paper, but it is too early to say if these schemes have been successful.

So far, the Deputy Director told us, medical health care has been a success story with the infant mortality rate drastically reduced. Education, on the other hand, has been a failure with a very high drop-out rate. Furthermore, poorly motivated teachers are reluctant to work in out-of-the-way places. Land development has had only moderate success and then only amongst the more settled Orang Asli.

While the avowed intention of the Department of Orang Asli affairs is to encourage the Orang Asli to become part of the Malay community, development and integration have not been as successful as hoped for. As one of the reasons for this, writings mention the Orang Asli suspicion of what they perceive as pressure on them from the Malays to become Muslims. The Deputy Director was quick to point out that the department did not force the Orang Asli to become Muslims. Although we had not brought up the subject of Islam, he obviously realised that conversion was implicit in the idea of the Orang Asli becoming a part of the Malay community. We did not put words in the mouths of the Orang Asli but none of the ones we met were remotely interested in converting to Islam which, apart from anything else, forbids the eating of wild pigs, squirrels, reptiles and amphibians, animals which have always been an important part of their diet. Any Orang Asli who became Muslims would, to a large extent, be relinquishing their own special way of life.

A wooden mask carved by the Mah Meri Orang Asli of Carey Island. It is thought the masks were originally used to conceal the identity of a sick person, thus fooling the evil spirits into leaving him/her.

9

Pests,
Pets
and
Jungle

B ang. Bash. Wallop. Buzz. Something enormous had zoomed in the window and was crashing uncontrollably around the room. We ducked as it flew past our heads and shot back to the fluorescent light. With a bang which threatened to break the tube, it fell, dazed, to the ground. A large, green beetle rolled over on to its legs and lumbered across the floor to hide under a chair. It was time to close the windows. Night was falling fast. We picked up the bewildered beetle, tossed it through the louvres and began to snap them shut. It was hot. We could have done with a cool breeze but we knew from experience that it was not worth it.

We had learned our lesson on our first night in the kampong. That evening too had been hot and after the last of our visiting neighbours had left with the fall of darkness we had switched on all the lights and, glasses of orange juice in our hands, slouched, panting, on the sofa. Until this point we had been staying in air-conditioned hotels. This was to be our first real tropical night. The walls, we noticed, were covered with insects but small lizards with an astonishing adhesive power were scuttling after them, stalking, pouncing, snapping and devouring them one after another. We watched bemused for a while as they competed with sharp, quarrelsome twitters for prime territory next to the lights. Then we realised that we too were being covered with insects as they flew in the window, hit the light and dropped bedazzled on to our laps, into our hair and down our necks. Jumping up to move we discovered that our empty glasses were under attack. Countless black ants swarmed over them, more arriving by the second from a file which stretched down the wall and across the floor. We rushed with our glasses to the kitchen and there discovered an enormous spider, the diameter of a jam-jar lid, lurking in the sink. A great deal of dexterity with a broom was required before it was persuaded to scurry out beneath the door into the garden.

Meanwhile the flying insect invasion was growing by the minute. Eventually we decided that the only way to escape the bombardment was to turn off the lights and go to bed. By this time the rooms were alive. We could have stocked an insect museum. There were brilliant green grasshoppers, winged ants, beetles of every colour, long-legged flies and winged and antennaed creatures of every description. Moths of varied hues clung to the walls. Some were tiny and pearly, others triangular, patterned with black and brown like streamlined military jets, others striped red and beige and a few small, delicate and a beautiful luminescent green. Though fascinated we were somewhat taken aback. Was this what nights in the tropics were to be like?

Our bed, when we finally reached it, was covered. The white sheets were swarming and, although we shook them off as best we could, we still felt insects crawling and wriggling about during the night. In addition, voracious mosquitoes dive-bombed, puncturing us even through the sheet we were hiding under. We had learned a few useful lessons. Next day we fixed mosquito netting over the air vents and from then on, after the fall of darkness, no matter how hot it was, we closed up the windows. Happily the insect population also decreased of its own accord as our occupation of the previously empty house drove them back outside. We bought coils and electric vapour-mat machines to ward off mosquitoes and we learned very quickly to wash our sticky glasses.

However, we never managed completely to expel the ants from the house. They nested under the flower pots, beneath the linoleum and in cracks in the walls. They burrowed spaces behind the tiles in the bathroom and colonised the underside of any convenient and stationary object. From here they would emerge in predatory files. Any unwashed crockery, spilt drops of food or fruit skins would, within minutes, be covered with swarms of the creatures, all collecting their tiny portions to carry back along the highway to their nests. We waged a constant war against them and even our food cupboard legs stood in bowls of water to keep them out. There were many varieties, all with their own special tastes and characteristics. The black ants enjoyed anything sugary as well as dead insects. Small red ants, with a ferocious bite but thankfully not given to colonising the interior of the house, preferred fatty and meaty titbits. Tiny ants ate anything and were not beyond giving human flesh a nip now and then. Large ants preferred a vegetarian diet and lived in holes in the garden while giant red ants, those with the worst bite of all, luckily kept to trees where they built bulky nests of large leaves bound together with silk-like secretions.

The fearsome-looking spiders which had terrified us at first, we eventually discovered to be harmless. The pregnant females carried white puff-ball-like egg sacs clutched to their abdomens and when these dropped the walls and ceilings were instantly covered with hundreds of minute spiders spreading out in all directions as they rushed for cover from the house lizards. Spiders have a special place for Malays because one is said to have saved the Prophet Mohammed from his enemies when he was hiding in a cave by spinning a web across the entrance. Concluding from the presence of the web that no one had recently entered, they did not bother to search for him there and he was able to escape.

Geckos, the little beige house lizards, are not so well thought of and it is an acceptable sport for young Malay boys to kill them on Friday nights. This is because the loud chiding chirps, from which their Malay name *chichak* is derived, are said to have attracted Mohammed's enemies to the cave in the first place and it was only the quick action of the spider which saved him.

We found these bulging-eyed, miniature crocodiles immensely useful. Every evening they would emerge from behind pictures and from holes in the roof to patrol the walls, ceilings and tables snatching up those of the insect swarms which appealed to their tastes. They would even tackle large moths and, if successful in catching them, would stagger about the walls, the flapping wings protruding from the sides of their mouths. Their gravity-defying methods of clinging and moving upside-down are apparently due to millions of minute hairs on their feet which catch in the tiniest of crevices. Even dead, they remain stuck to the wall. Occasionally, however, usually in the course of a scuffle or an amorous chase the geckos can lose their grip. Once one fell on a visitor's neck and he was still yelping from the fright when an Indian in the room exclaimed that he should be pleased as this meant he would soon receive some money.

Geckos, if frightened, have an unusual way of escaping from their pursuers. The first time we saw this we were as startled as the lizard itself which, in its haste to escape from us, dropped its tail. We watched with horrified fascination as this discarded appendage continued to wriggle and squirm for a further five minutes, nature's way of distracting a would-be attacker.

Geckos were of particular help in ridding the house of flying termites. "Invasion!" – the call generally came from the cook of the evening. These termites would, on certain evenings and usually after rain, arise from their nests to provide us with an aerial show as the swooping, darting and somersaulting birds feasted upon them. Later, however, hordes of them would converge on the lights, wriggling through the louvres and into the house to fall, drop their wings and mate. We wished they would find a more suitable spot for courting than our soups and stews. Unable to pick them out we simply stirred them in and ate our protein-enhanced meal in semi-darkness to avoid further bombardments.

Another food-spoiler was a tiny dull beetle which, when touched, released a strong musky smell which clung to the fingers and hair and ruined sauces. Our floors in the evening were generally littered with small, shiny, black beetles and these delighted Liam when he learned to crawl. He would sit under the light, pounce on any that fell and stuff them into his mouth. Many times we rescued them from him, their bodies mashed, their legs still wriggling.

We had lodgers. Manfred was with us for several months and inhabited the roof space. We could hear him up there thumping, banging and scuffling, no doubt terrorising the resident geckos, but only a few times did we catch a glimpse of him. He was a beautifully striped, two-foot-long, black and yellow monitor lizard with a constantly flicking tongue but was understandably shy as he is considered a delicacy by Indians and Chinese.

Sammy the house shrew was our favourite. He was a strange rodent with a long, pointed snout, tiny eyes and a piercing chirrup when alarmed. This slow, bumbling little animal finds its way around, like a bat, largely by echolocation. It is harmless to humans, carries no disease and eats up cockroaches. We were fond of ours but, as his large droppings had a rather unpleasant musky smell, we eventually caught him and took him away to find a new home.

Unwelcome squatters we had in plenty. Although expelled daily, a series of great warty toads would squirm their way under the door when we weren't looking and hide in the most unexpected places. One particularly liked a slipper and hid in it during thunderstorms. Another, seemingly bent on self-education, spent its time in a bag of books, while another preferred the laundry basket. It even got put into the washing machine and was lucky to be rescued before the cycle started. One was so devoted to us it hopped on to the back seat of the car and travelled with us to Ipoh. We only discovered it, panting from the scorching heat, after several hours. We poured on water and popped it into the bushes but it later found its way into our friends' house and settled down there to a new life as their resident toad.

Our unkempt, weedy garden was the habitat of a variety of creatures. Lizards with extremely long tails and fierce-looking jagged spines occasionally entered the house by mistake, skating panic-stricken on the linoleum before we brushed them out again. One even jumped down the toilet in its terror and had to be pulled out. These lizards can change colour but not for the purpose of camouflage. The males adopt a pinkish blush with a black blotch on their heads when courting and when frightened they turn blackish all over.

We encountered relatively few snakes around our house although guests from France got a terrible fright when a long, brown snake slithered in the front door. We'd barely had time to gasp when, realising it had taken a wrong turning, it slid back outside. We never saw it again but our friends left convinced that we lived in mortal danger. By and large the only snakes we ever saw were dead and flattened on the roads though, judging from the frequency with which they are killed in this way, there are plenty of them around. Most snakes are very secretive and, detecting a person's presence, will move away long before they are spotted. They have no more desire for a confrontation than we do especially as they are likely to get the worst of it. In any case only five of the 111 Malaysian species are poisonous enough to pose a serious danger and only the king cobra is unafraid of humans.

The insects never ceased to surprise us. Although they were camouflaged almost perfectly, we sometimes found stick insects looking exactly like brown twigs. Green praying mantises hopped on to our window louvres to observe us in their supercilious manner, their front legs, flattened to resemble the sleeves of a cassock, raised in piety. An enormous black insect, which we named Helibee, had its permanent perch on a fence post and would spend the day making sorties in search of food. It got quite agitated and flew around buzzing if its helipad was approached, even occasionally chasing away birds. Despite its fearful appearance, it seemed harmless.

Odd leaf-cutting flies attacked the mango trees which our landlord had planted. After inserting their eggs into a vein in the leaf they would patiently saw across it near the upper end, thus allowing the egg-bearing portion to drop to the ground. The eggs eventually hatched, the larvae developed in the soil and a new batch of flies emerged.

Inside the house lone wasps would construct tough nests from mud, buzzing in and out with portions of 'mortar'. Inside each chamber they laid an elongated egg and alongside they stored a dead fly or spider for the hatched larva to feed on before it was ready to burrow its way out.

Beautiful butterflies and moths are numerous in Malaysia and many varieties visited our garden, flitting in and out of the windows as they fancied. Their caterpillars gorged themselves on our potted plants. These greedy creatures took as many forms as their parents; some were hairy, others smooth, many were colourful but most had excellent camouflage and were only detected when we noticed the plant had been almost eaten away. One day droppings the size of hazelnuts appeared at the back door beneath the wild guava tree. On looking round to see what animal might have produced them we were amazed to find a gigantic silvery-green caterpillar, about five inches long, chomping its way rapidly through a leaf. This was, we discovered later, the larva of the atlas moth, an enormous brown, white and yellow beauty with a ten-inch wing-span.

At night, while the bull-frogs in our cistern chorused discordantly, the cicadas screeched monotonously, the nightjars klonked and the little owl coo-ooed from its fence post perch, the garden was lit by fireflies. The rear ends of these little beetles blinked with a greenish radiance as they signalled for mates. Sometimes they found their way into the house and when we turned off the lamp to go to sleep we would find a little night-light quietly glowing on the ceiling or winking around the room.

Many birds lived around the house. Brilliant blue kingfishers perched on the fence posts, bee-eaters hawked insects from the electricity wires and woodpeckers scrambled up the wooden telegraph posts. Sparrows nested and quarrelled in the eaves and on quiet afternoons weren't beyond hopping around the kitchen in search of titbits. Strangely, in a country where the European house sparrow is absent, these tree sparrows, normally quite shy in Europe, have adopted the cheekier role of their cousins. We were used to their intrusions but were startled one day by a bird flying like a rocket straight through the back door and into the spare room. On investigating we found a bird known as a spiderhunter flapping about entangled in webs. Although its family was easily identifiable from its fine, extremely long, curved bill we were keen to discover which species it was and quickly consulted our bird book. There was no doubt. Under 'little spiderhunter' we found an apt description: "Frequents lower storey through which it flies at high speed"!

Animals too wandered into the house on exploratory jaunts. Not long after we moved in a lone little baby goat trotted up. It circled the house several times, peering shyly in the door, and finally tiptoed in on tiny hooves to explore the house room by room. A few days later a small chicken did exactly the same thing while mother hen clucked anxiously outside. Next, a very confident sparrow hopped round on the same course while we sat watching it. By the time a kitten came exploring we were rapidly coming to the conclusion that our neighbours, by now a little more reticent about looking around our house in person and having noticed the soft spot we had for animals and birds, were calling upon the powers of the *bomoh* to endow them with non-human forms in order to continue their investigations.

* * *

We loved the rainforest and went there as often as possible. The mountains which dominate the centre of the peninsula are thickly forested and we lived only a few miles from the jungle fringe. Unfortunately the forest there was under 24-hour curfew, the security forces fearing that the beleaguered communist guerrillas, still lingering on in small numbers from the time of the Emergency, could too easily receive supplies from sympathisers. We were warned repeatedly against venturing beyond the rubber estates.

We were curious, however, and one quiet Sunday morning we took our motorbike and followed one of the estate paths to its end. We had just begun to enjoy our first taste of the forest when a rumble of vehicles sent us scurrying for cover. We had heard that soldiers in curfew areas shoot first and ask questions later. Shaking with fear we crouched in the prickly bushes as the convoy of trucks came closer. Then, to our great relief, it passed on along the rough track. We fled back to our bike and never entered the curfew zone again.

Our first real experience of the primary tropical rainforest was in Taman Negara, the peninsula's only national park which occupies 1,677 square miles (4,343 square kilometres) in the centre of the country. To reach it we had to make our way to Kuala Tembeling, a small village on the banks of the wide, brown Tembeling river. Leaving all other vehicles behind, we got into the long, wooden boat which was to take us three hours upriver to the park headquarters. It was a delightful journey. Little wooden houses perched high on the banks with steps down to the river. Children from them splashed and dived in the water and waved as we sped by. Elsewhere great black buffaloes lounged, their pale foreheads and strong, curved horns just above the surface. After we reached the park boundaries the river narrowed a little and signs of habitation dwindled. All around was forest. Tall trees covered the hills, others reached out from the banks and we spotted kingfishers with enormous, long, orange beaks perched on overhanging branches. Pairs of straw-headed bulbuls flitted close to the water landing with a wonderful, rich, burbling chorus. A five-foot monitor lizard slid down the bank and into the water, fooling us into believing it was a crocodile. Although native to Malaysia and once common, crocodiles are no longer found in the Tembeling. Indeed they are not often encountered in the peninsula now although they are still a menace to some of the riverine dwellers of Borneo.

After arriving at the headquarters, a collection of offices and chalets on a grassy bank high above the river, we headed directly along the nearest path into the forest. Immense trees soared heavenward on perfectly straight, unbranched trunks while at lower levels shrubs and creepers wrestled for space. The dark, giant leaves of palms unfurled among the trees and the serrated fronds of luxuriant ferns patterned the sides of the path and hung above our heads. Thick stands of bamboo rustled mysteriously in the still air. Huge, brown leaves, hunched like sleeping animals, littered the ground.

Suddenly there was a loud crashing. Something big was heading towards us through the silent forest. We looked at each other in disbelief. Then along the path stamped two men, huge rucksacks on their backs, their legs covered with scratches and leech bites.

"Gunung Tahan," they called as they rushed past us. Having just climbed the peninsula's highest peak, 7,174 feet (2,187 metres), an arduous round trip of nine days through the park, they were obviously in a great hurry for a cold shower.

Next morning we set off early to climb nearby Bukit Teresek, 1,130 feet (344 metres). We made slow progress — there were just too many things to examine along the way. Chief among these were termites, tiny creatures apparently like ants though of a different family, which poured in their thousands across the path and along tree roots in a moving black stream intent on some unseen mission. Living in large, complex, communal mounds, up to half a million strong, these busy insects perform an essential function in the forest by helping to break down dead trees and plants. They are also a major source of food for pangolins, shrews and other insectivores.

Bird-watching also slowed us down. Although the forest was sometimes completely silent, at other times we scarcely knew where to look next as they arrived in waves. Over 600 species of birds inhabit the peninsula and although often difficult to spot in the thick forest, sightings are invariably rewarding. There are skulking brown babblers and cheeky bulbuls, enormous eagles and tiny flowerpeckers, bright-green leafbirds, blue flycatchers, luminous red and yellow minivets, brilliant fairy bluebirds, tiny lorikeets which prefer to hang upside-down from the tops of trees, tailorbirds which stitch leaves together to make nests, drongos with long fluttering tail streamers and huge glamorous pheasants which strut about the forest floor.

By the time we neared the top of the hill the noise which had drawn us there had long since ceased. As dawn broke it had begun, a chorus of resonant whoops, hoots and exuberant burbles rising, falling and leap-frogging with the rapidly increasing light. These were the calls of a group of white-handed gibbons, which frequented the hill, a sound which was to become for us one of the loveliest of the forest. We still hoped to see some and indeed we could hear them crashing through the branches not far off. Unlike monkeys these apes do not scramble along on all fours but hang and swing from their enormously long arms. We crept on as silently as we could and then, suddenly, spotted one just above us on a fruiting tree. We raised our binoculars slowly to examine this tremendously powerful creature with its almost human appearance. It had dark brown fur contrasting with white hands and face. Hanging leisurely from one long arm, it stuffed fruit and leaves into its mouth with the opposite hand. The strain of peering upwards became too much and one of us made a movement. The gibbon whirled round and on seeing us immediately leapt away. Then, to our surprise, it stopped and turned round again as if to have a better look at the bothersome creatures below, before crashing away through the trees, swinging rapidly hand over hand and hurling itself across the perilous abysses between trees. Within seconds all was silent.

On the other side of the hill we discovered a look-out point with a wooden seat and plonked ourselves down to gaze out over the forest. The view was magnificent. As far as the eye could see there were trees. No towns or villages, no palm oil or rubber plantations, just pure, untouched forest. In the distance the hills were bluish. Nearby the forest, seen from above, was a gorgeous brocade of every imaginable shade of green and an infinite variety of textures. New foliage was a bright pea-green. Older trees looked like purplish broccoli. Tall iron-grey trunks thrust through the canopy gaps and here and there were patches of brilliant scarlet or purple where some of the trees were in bloom.

Soon we became aware of a persistent loud honking, not unlike a domestic goose. Squealing with excitement we pulled up our binoculars in time to see a rhinoceros hornbill. This four-foot long black and white bird puffed slowly across in front of us, the steam-train noise from its underwing air sacs audible even from a distance and the curved, red, horned casque above its massive bill clearly visible. No sooner had it glided into a treetop than another, following the same path, crossed to join it.

It was our first sighting of a rhinoceros hornbill, perhaps the most famous and distinctive of Malaysia's many birds. There are ten species of hornbill in the country, most with huge casques attached to their heavy beaks. Apart from the pied hornbills which gather in noisy flocks, they are difficult to spot as most inhabit the upper canopies of thick forest. The unique chuffing noise from the wing sacs of many species, however, draws attention to their presence.

Their calls are also loud and distinctive, the most remarkable being that of the helmeted hornbill. Starting with a series of poops which gradually increase in frequency it ends with a maniacal laugh that rings out through the forest for miles. This bird was widely hunted in former times for its casque which was highly valued as a medium for intricate and often beautiful carving. Although its call was a familiar sound of the forest we saw this bird only once, flying high above us. It was unmistakable, a huge four-footer with a 20-inch elongated tail feather streaming out behind it.

Hornbills have peculiar nesting habits. When the female is ready to lay she enters a hole in a tree which the male then plasters over with mud leaving only a small gap through which he pokes titbits of food. This is thought to protect the eggs and nestlings from predators. After about three months, while the eggs incubate and hatch and the fledglings develop, she breaks down the barrier and emerges.

The most striking feature of the rainforest is its height. The tallest trees, mainly of the dipterocarp family, grow to about 150 and even 200 feet. They are characterised by their immense, straight trunks lifting a crown of foliage to a height where the most light may be obtained. In fact keen competition for light to a large extent determines the arrangement of a tropical rainforest where optimum conditions exist for growth – an abundance of rain and high temperatures all the year round. There are at least 3,000 species of trees not to mention countless more plants. All of them need light but have devised different methods for obtaining it. The dipterocarps stretch themselves high. Creepers, lianas and vines twine their way upwards using other plants for support. Smaller plants on the forest floor, where only 3 per cent of the light penetrates, have adapted themselves to the poor conditions and arrange their leaves in a horizontal plane avoiding overlap to obtain maximum benefit. Epiphytic ferns and orchids needing plentiful light attach themselves to loftier plants, often in the crook of a tree branch, but obtain their own nutriment independently of the host plant, trapping old fallen leaves around their roots or even within their own fronds. The strangler fig begins as an epiphyte on the upper branches of an unfortunate tree. One by one it sends aerial roots to the ground. These increase and thicken, eventually fusing to encase the host tree which dies, leaving the independent fig high in the canopy with a substantial 'trunk' of interwoven roots.

The soils of a tropical rainforest are poor in nutrients as they have only a thin layer of organic matter. Due to the constantly high temperatures, the rate of decomposition is fast but the nutrients released are quickly utilised by plants and, as there is no quiescent winter period, a deep humus level does not have a chance to develop. Thus the roots of the trees, to derive maximum benefit, must be very shallow and many of the tallest grow enormous buttresses, up to eight feet tall and a few inches wide, along the lateral roots to help support the bole. Other trees suspend stilt roots from many feet above ground level which eventually grow down and anchor in the earth below.

The competition for nutrients is fierce. Some plants are parasites, extracting nourishment from other plants with their special penetrating roots. Abundant fungi depend on both dead and living organic matter and algae, lichens and mosses colonise large leaves. Some plants are even carnivorous and dangle a number of graceful and enticing little pots or pitchers to lure insects. These receptacles, usually about four inches high and provided with a little raised lid to keep out excessive rain, are filled with a fluid containing digestive enzymes. Insects, attracted by a secretion at the mouth of the pitcher, invariably slip into the fluid and their rapidly-dissolved bodies are absorbed as food by the plant.

The variety of growth in the tropics is stupendous. Because the diverse species are so numerous the density of their occurrence is very low. As many as 60 types of tree can be found within one acre. If, however, the tall canopy trees are cleared a very different type of vegetation grows up. The shade-adapted plants which usually inhabit the forest floor are unable to thrive in the open sunlight. Fast-growing and light-loving plants with high densities and swift reproduction systems such as grasses and shrubs, stunted by the normal dim forest conditions, flourish in abundance. The result is an impenetrable tangle quite different from the normal forest under storey which, although difficult to pass through is by no means the dense mass it is popularly believed to be. If the clearing is a small one, tree seedlings will later establish themselves in both the shade of the secondary growth and of the spreading foliage of the adjacent trees. They will eventually emerge to fill the canopy gap although full regeneration may take 100 years or more. If the clearing is extensive, however, the nutrients will be washed quickly away from the exposed soil and the tree seedlings will perish in the scorching heat. The tropical rainforest has evolved to its present state over 130 million years. Once extensively cleared it cannot regenerate itself. The complex interdependency of plants, animals and birds is a delicate one and when one element is destroyed the whole must suffer.

Of the larger mammals — tigers, leopards, elephants, rhinoceroses and seladangs (a kind of wild cattle also known by the name gaur) — many have now been severely diminished in numbers as their natural habitat has decreased. Sumatran rhinoceroses are on the verge of extinction; only 40 at most are believed to still exist while tigers are estimated to number less than 500. Only 20 years ago there were 3,000.

Many forest animals are very shy and, with their acute powers of hearing and smell, move well out of sight before even the stealthiest human has approached. The best chance of seeing the more common mammals, many of which are nocturnal, is to spend a night in a hide. We managed to do this

a few times. Our hopes were particularly high at Kumbang Hide where a salt
lick at the edge of the clearing was reputed to attract tapir, a strange,
snouted animal the size of a pony with a black head and rump and a central
white saddle.

On clambering into the hide we found two Swedes already waiting,
patiently and silently. We settled down beside them at the window and
gazed expectantly out at the empty clearing. What magnificent beasts had
our noisy approach to the hide scared away? We didn't dare ask the silent
watchers. The clearing was empty, devoid of even a flutter or a chirp. Then,
suddenly, a pure white apparition fleeted across before our astonished eyes.
We did not have time to pick up our binoculars. It was gone, but we knew
what we'd seen — an Asian paradise flycatcher. The males with long ten-
inch fluttering streamers have two phases, one brown and the other pure
white. The latter was what we had seen and as we searched around we
caught a final glimpse of its ethereal white form flitting away through the
trees like a ghost of the forest.

Darkness fell. Eagerly we readied ourselves for the evening performance.
Every 15 minutes we switched on our torch, shining the beam first into the
tree tops and gradually approaching the clearing so as not to startle any
visitors. After an hour of inactivity one of the Swedes decided that the smell
of burning mosquito coils must be responsible for keeping all the panthers,
tapirs and rhinoceroses away from the salt lick. The coils were all extin-
guished. Now at last we had wildlife to keep us company even if it was only
around the ankles.

Something rustled. Our drooping heads swivelled. There was definitely
something large in the vicinity of the hide. A torch check on the clearing
revealed nothing. Was it in the nearby trees? Alert, we listened. It was
raining now and drips plopped from the foliage. Another rustle. It sounded
very close — possibly even right inside the hide. Then suddenly, with a sharp
squeak, something rushed across the ledge in front of our noses. All four of
us leapt backwards and the bench crashed over on to the floor. Torches
flashed on and the culprit, an enormous rat, could be seen dashing under a
bunk.

"A jungle rat," proclaimed one of our Swedish companions knowledge-
ably.

Ah! Genuine wildlife. There was at least no shortage of these rodents
inside the hide. We realised that an army of them had joined us, drawn by
our bags of sandwiches — probably a regular attraction. We lit a small candle
and placed it by our feet to keep the rats at bay. The Swedes looked
askance. We stared out at the clearing and momentarily imagined a large
rock to be an elephant.

Suddenly a loud clang from the rubbish bin underneath the hide had us
all rushing for the door. Just saving ourselves from pitching headlong out

of the 50-foot-high hide, we caught a brief glimpse of a small cat-like creature bounding away and all sagely concluded that it was a civet cat. There then followed a prolonged period with everyone absorbed, under discreet torchlight, in their Malaysian mammal books in an effort to work out which of the many varieties of civet cat found in Malaysia it could possibly have been. Eventually books thudded shut with sighs of frustration at the impossibility of the task and we attempted to revive our flagging interest in the clearing outside.

The rain increased to a drizzle, diminishing the chances of thirsty animals visiting for a drink, while the dense cloud cover ensured minimum possible light from a waning moon by which to see them anyway. We decided on a shift system and non-watchers tumbled gratefully into their bunks.

It would be difficult to think of a less stimulating experience. Cupping hands behind ears to catch any hint of movement, and staring wide-eyed into solid blackness, one could only attempt imaginary re-runs of favourite David Attenborough clips. However, even imagination failed and all that remained was to patiently count away the minutes to the next torch check. But the clearing proved empty yet again. Back to darkness and the monotonous pattering rain drops.

The sky was at last lightening. Trees became dimly visible and those sleeping got up. Suddenly a huge kite-like shape sailed across the clearing and landed with a whump just above the hide. Sticking our heads out of the hide, we were in time to see a large red squirrel clamber out of view. It was a flying squirrel, one of the many creatures which have evolved 'wings' to equip them for arboreal movement in the forest thus saving themselves the trouble of a long trip to the ground. Some lizards as well as colugos (so-called flying lemurs although they are not lemurs at all) have also developed the ability to 'fly'. Their wings are actually flaps of membraneous skin between front and back legs which can be spread wide, like sails, when they wish to glide.

By eight o'clock in the morning we had given up our watch and were packing noisily to leave when our attention was drawn back to the clearing by a short, hoarse, dog-like bark. There, standing in the middle, were two barking deer, rich russet-coloured animals, their faces finely lined with black, two short pointed horns on the head of the male. We watched these infrequently-seen deer with delight as they roamed peacefully around the clearing.

Later in the day we were lucky once more. Sitting quietly on a rise to eat our sandwiches we caught a glimpse of a small dog-like form trotting across the path below on spindly legs and tiny hooves. It was not a dog but a mouse deer which, though resembling a small deer, is actually more closely related to a camel! This animal is quite common but being mainly nocturnal it is not often seen. Malay folklore is full of stories in which this little creature out-smarts the mighty carnivores.

Our return through the forest to the headquarters was not entirely carefree. On previous trips to Taman Negara part of our enjoyment of the place had been derived from its remoteness from the outside world, its timeless immunity from people and their machines and the knowledge that, as a national park, this forest could never be destroyed. We had therefore been thoroughly dismayed, in early 1982, to learn that the government was planning to build a hydro-electric dam across the Tembeling river which would flood huge areas of the park. The percentage of the park to be lost, they argued, would be a small one but wildlife enthusiasts were quick to point out that this small percentage was in fact a large amount of the lowland forest which harbours the vast majority of plant, animal, insect and bird species. This forest is becoming increasingly scarce in Malaysia due to the high quality of its hardwoods and its accessibility to loggers.

The debate was taken up by the newspapers, petitions were signed, surveys were organised and to our great relief, early in 1983, the government announced that, due to economic cutbacks, plans for the dam were to be shelved. This time Taman Negara had been granted a reprieve but the park's vulnerability had been demonstrated and it is still not clear if plans for the construction of the dam have been permanently abandoned. As the only extensive, fully-protected area of rainforest in the peninsula, its survival is essential for preservation to have any meaning.

Malaysia, including Borneo, is the location of the oldest, undisturbed tropical rainforest in the world. For 130 million years it dominated the landscape, only insignificant patches of cultivation being won away from it. In the 20th century, however, the wholesale clearing of huge areas for plantations and more efficient logging methods have been pushing back the forest at unimaginable rates. In 1977 680,000 acres of forest were being logged annually and the Deputy Prime Minister announced that if uncontrolled exploitation was to continue the timber resources would be depleted within 12 years. This complete devastation of the forest could be avoided if the valuable trees were removed selectively and the gaps replanted and allowed to regenerate. But the profit is quicker if the forest is carelessly felled and not many of those in the trade are concerned about how the depletion of resources will affect future generations let alone the well-being of the wildlife. There have been attempts to curb logging but even in forest reserve areas it goes on illegally and largely unimpeded.

Already the effects of forest depletion are being felt. The rainfall of the country has decreased markedly and when the rain does fall, floods are commonplace. There is insufficient forest cover to 'hold' the rainfall and as the coastal areas cannot cope with the water, severe flooding is a regular feature of low-lying towns. Furthermore, tons of soil from exposed, cleared areas are washed down rivers and into the sea.

Yet, despite the many warning signs, the destruction goes on. Although we can be thankful that so much of the interior is mountainous and economically unviable for logging and agriculture, it is the lowland forest — that which is the most diverse and the most unique and on which most of Malaysia's endangered flora and fauna depends — which is so tragically vulnerable. With its essential gene pools, its vital pharmacological resources and its vast, as yet untapped, potential not to mention its aesthetic beauty, it is in great danger. Once destroyed, it can never be replaced.

A Malay civet cat. (Photo by S. C. Bisserot, courtesy of the Royal Geographical Society)

Tree fern in the Cameron Highlands.

10
A Peninsular Circuit

Then August holidays had just begun. The East-West Highway had recently been opened and for the first time the two coasts of the peninsula were linked in the north by a road cutting across the mountain chain a little to the south of the Thai border. We decided to make an exploratory circuit.

The morning was clear and sunny. The road was busy. As we drove out of the kampong an old Indian ice cream seller pedalled laboriously past shouting encouragement to himself, his dark face, under grey hair, screwed up against the sun, his loaded metal box behind him. Each day, rain or shine, he cycled ten miles to a Chinese New Village and back, his reward dependent on the whims of the children and the indulgences of their mothers, his advertisement a jangling bell.

We turned on to the main road. Traffic raced past. Express buses swerved and weaved, apparently determined to reach their destinations in record-breaking time. Trucks ground their gears and gushed plumes of black, oily exhaust. Cars passed on blind corners. Not a chance was to be missed, not a moment lost, for these Malaysian drivers, so easy-going, so slow-moving in their daily lives, are attacked, at the wheels of their cars, by a great and urgent hunger for speed.

Suddenly the pace slowed and brake lights went on. Those slow to notice swerved to left and right. A wooden cart had joined the road. Two placid white bullocks with painted horns ambled forward, the dung-laden cart creaking behind them. Perched in front, an old blue-turbaned Sikh muttered exhortations into his long, white beard, apparently oblivious to the chaos he was creating. The cars jockeyed for position again. One or two sneaked past on the inside lane, the rutted mud shoulder. A taxi pulled out, apparently unaware of the oncoming express bus. It tried to pass but could not make it. At the last minute it dropped back, the cars behind braking to give it space. For that is the rule of the Malaysian speedway. The risk-taker is accommodated. There is no place for temper or principles, never mind the highway carnage which results.

A small truck rollicked past leaving behind an overpowering odour. "Durians," we stated simultaneously. The back was filled with this huge fruit, a contented man snoozing fakir-like on their thick thorns, no doubt sated with their flesh, intoxicated by their stench and happily anticipating the profits he would earn. For the durian induces a seasonal madness in Malaysians, inciting these languid people almost to passion. Stalls line the roadside and here the durian acts as an equaliser, a uniter of races. Motor scooters, Volvos and bicycles all halt by the rows of dangling fruits. The durian-testing squat is adopted. Discussion is grave. The art of selecting the perfect specimen is a fine one and must be approached with serious intent. It is weighed in the hand and gently shaken, ears alert for the rattle of a seed. The thick rind is scrutinised for imperfections or cracks. The spikes

105

must be of a certain diameter, the skin of the correct hue and most importantly, the smell of an overpowering pungency; for this notorious fruit stinks. The taste of the creamy flesh surrounding the huge inner seeds has been likened to that of peaches and cream – eaten in the toilet. Indeed, for those who can ignore the stench, the thick, custardy flesh can become an addiction and, throwing caution to the wind, the converted will consume durian after durian, unconcerned with the almost certain stomach-aches to follow. The durian is the supremely 'heaty' food, the epitome of the yin earth element. It must on no account be consumed with alcohol, the supremely 'heaty' drink, the combination, we were assured, being fatal. Instead, the 'cooling' mangosteen fruit, its seasonal companion, makes a perfect match.

The durian grows high on a tall, stately, forest tree, the fruit developing directly out of the branches and when ripe dropping to the ground, usually at night. It must not be picked and during the season trees will be guarded by their owners ready to retrieve the fallen produce. Protein rich, it is consumed by elephants and even tigers, given the chance. It is also said to be an aphrodisiac: "When the durian falls the sarong rises," say the Malays, but one can only hope both parties have partaken as the foul smell remains with the consumer, returning in frequent belches and oozing from the sweat pores.

We journeyed on. A desert of white sand stretched to the left, the legacy of opencast tin extraction. Opposite, a cleared hillside of bright pink laterite was gouged with deep gullies as the fragile, unclothed soil surrendered itself to passing downpours and eloped to the sea.

Our first destination was Batu Gajah. On the way we peered up to our left at Kellie's castle, an incomplete turreted Gothic folly from the days of the white planters – one man's desperate attempt to please a bored but ambitious wife. We had visited it once, wading across the river at the buffalo crossing and clambering up the overgrown hill, the great sweeping stone staircase now all but lost beneath tangled scrub. It stood forlornly, four storeys high at one corner, complete with ballroom and empty lift-shaft. An anarchy of intruding vegetation mocked the relief designs of disciplined tendrils on the white stuccoed walls. Gracefully colonnaded corridors were ambushed by greenery. An entire grove flourished on a roof, the thick, smooth, roots twining and merging as they reached for the ground. Nature triumphed over the vanity of Mr Kellie-Smith who, in his search of Europe for a suitable lift, died in distant Lisbon. An old Tamil man searched the grounds for wild chillies. A young boy grazed his buffaloes beneath the walls. They did not remember when it was constructed or know who had built it. They shrugged. It had always been there. It provided shelter from the rain.

Our goal at the moment was the Batu Gajah Game Department, our quest the black-crowned night heron. We stopped a trio of policemen. The Indian stepped forward proud to use his English. Yes, he knew the Game Department.

"Up the hill." His head waggled with certainty. "It is on the right. You cannot miss it."

We did miss it. It was on the left. The official at the door surveyed us with amazement as we drove up. On seeing baby Liam, however, his face brightened. Our young son was plucked from our arms and passed delightedly around the dozen or so male employees, set down to roam their enormous empty desk tops and finally whisked to the door of a barred and locked cell inside which stood a rack of rifles, a mound of severed elephants' feet and a collection of antlers.

When the excitement had died down and we had satisfied all questions as to our abode, employment and the price of our car, we explained our visit. We wanted permission to visit the bird sanctuary at Kuala Gula, to find the nesting colony of herons deep in the coastal mangrove swamps.

A map was pulled out and everyone crowded round. The coast of Perak was located, routes were discussed and it was decided we should go to Kuala Gula.

This much we had deduced for ourselves. We tried to be patient. "But we need a boat to find the birds."

The government department officials looked puzzled. It appeared that none of them had ever been there, much less given any thought to the place.

"There is a ranger at Kuala Gula. He has a boat."

We brightened. "But the boat is out of order," someone volunteered.

"And you will need permission," another added.

"From whom?"

"From the Department in Kuala Lumpur."

But they had directed us to Batu Gajah.

"When you have permission we can contact the ranger and arrange a boat."

"But you said the boat was out of order."

Exhausted by logical cul-de-sacs, we gave up. The men suggested we come back the next morning to see their boss who was at a meeting, but we had a wedding to attend in Ipoh. We decided just to go to Kuala Gula and see what happened.

"What do you all do here?" we asked as we prepared to leave. The throng, obviously in no hurry to return to the void of their empty desks, had clustered at the door.

"We look after the sanctuary," one man answered pointing across the road to a scrubby looking area, apparently a bird reserve.

"And the herons," another chipped in. "The herons at Kuala Gula."

* * *

Our next port of call was Ipoh where one of our local Sikh buffalo herders was to be married. As arranged, we met his brother near a roundabout.

"I will show you the way," he shouted and, jumping into a car laden with family members, zoomed off. We did our best to follow him but other cars got between us. Suddenly we lost him. We drove in the direction we thought he had taken and then spotted before us a car-load of turbans. It turned left and right ending up in an obscure housing estate.

"Welcome." A rotund Sikh with a neat beard-net ushered us to the lines of decorated tables outside the house and settled us in two of the chairs. "You are with Jasbeer's party?"

Jasbeer? We looked puzzled.

"The groom. From Kampar?"

Our buffalo herder was not Jasbeer. His name was Pretam. We searched the crowd for his familiar face but the young groom, spruce in pale suit, shirt and tie, coloured wool pompoms decorating his wrist, was not Pretam. Our mistake dawned on us. We jumped up apologetically.

"I'm afraid we've ended up at the wrong wedding. We were following a car . . ."

The man laughed. "Well I cannot help you to find your friend's wedding but if you wish to remain with us you are most welcome, most welcome indeed."

The story circulated among the crowd. Whiskered faces beamed beneath multi-coloured turbans and we were pressed to resume our seats and feast on the sugary tea and cakes.

After the ceremony we chatted to the man who had befriended us. We asked him what his job was.

"Oh, a bit of this and that. I'm a taxi operator." But he owned the taxis. Others drove them.

"Also I do a little money-lending," he added, "and sell Singer products."

"That must keep you busy," we commented.

"Oh, those are just my sidelines. I work as a security guard eight hours a day. I am a typical Malaysian," he laughed, "with a finger in many pies."

* * *

Next morning we collected our friend Chong Peng and headed north to Taiping and then towards the coast. The coastal area was thick with oil palm estates. The dark, squat, scaly-trunked trees brooded along either side of rutted, unsignposted mud tracks, their sinister aspect enlivened only by numerous kingfishers which perched on wires and dived brilliantly into the fetid perimeter ditches. We peered into the gloom and could just discern shadowy workers harvesting the huge bundles of heavy fruit among the dim arcades.

A bumping, exhaust-crashing eternity later we found ourselves at the village of Kuala Gula. Grubby Chinese children surrounded the car jostling for a glimpse of the strange white baby. Chong Peng went to make enquiries about the heronry. The ranger, he reported, lived in another part of the village, the Malay section.

The village, strung along the waterside, was split in two. The Chinese houses were clustered around the harbour, the inhabitants fishing for prawns and searching the mud flats at low tide for crabs and shellfish. They had their own shops and eating *kedais*, their Chinese-language primary school and their harbour temple. Further up the channel the Malay houses stood, swathed in bougainvillaea. The fishermen here derived their income from government-sponsored fish farms. They caught a few fish, popped them in and harvested the offspring. They rarely went to sea. Living an existence completely separate from their neighbours, they had their own shops, their school and their mosque. They spoke only Malay and the Chinese spoke next to none. The two communities never mixed and, while sharing the same village, could scarcely communicate. Indeed, they rarely had the need.

The Malay ranger was an amiable man and although about to go off duty, readily volunteered to accompany us. However, as we couldn't use the official boat we had to return to the Chinese harbour to hire one privately. The ranger couldn't help us here. He spoke no Chinese, knew none of the residents and in fact had never set foot in this part of the village. We were lucky to have Chong Peng with us.

The harbour did not look directly on to the open sea. In fact for much of the western fringe of the peninsula it is impossible to say where exactly the coastline is. Mangroves blend into the sea, reclaiming land from it as their roots build up accumulations of silt and mud. At high tide the trunks of these salt-resistant forests appear to rise directly from the sea. At low tide their roots are revealed, branching out and down from the trunk, splayed stilts which, when uncovered, absorb essential oxygen from the air. At their base hundreds of brown fish known as mud skippers leap and twist on the slime with the aid of specially developed fins. Numerous feuding fiddler crabs scuttle back and forth on sorties from their burrows waving their solitary, useless, outsized, pink nippers.

Our boat chugged away from the harbour. It was a beautifully clear day. The sky was a brochure-blue and light sparkled on the choppy waves. Stretches of light-green foliage marked the mangrove clumps and their roots could just be seen straddling the slapping waves as the high tide rushed in. The ranger directed the boat from channel to channel. Already, the boatmen told Chong Peng, they were unsure of their bearings. This particular mangrove maze has baffled police for years in their search for a notorious local pirate who hides his boats and his henchmen there, demanding regular protection money from the local fishermen. But the ranger knew his way. He led us first to observe a collection of adjutant and milky storks, perched heavily on the fragile branches waiting for the full moon tide to retreat and allow them back to their feeding grounds. The boat engine startled them and they took off on huge wings to wheel in elegant circles far above our heads.

An hour of scudding over the choppy waves of the open sea brought us to the heronry. We realised then that the ranger's company was essential — the boatmen had no idea where to go. The Malay, however, after careful scrutiny of the mangrove fringe, directed them to a point indistinguishable, as far as we could see, from any other for several miles in either direction.

We tied the boat to a branch. From here we had to walk, or rather, slither. The murky water was thigh deep. The thick, soft mud oozed over our shoes and threatened to suck them from our feet. As we moved, the water turned black from the churned up slime and a noxious sulphury smell was released. Eventually we had to remove our shoes for fear of losing them and proceed barefoot, ever anxious about what our groping toes might encounter in the unseen depths. But the mud was soft and the only signs of life were mottled, purple crabs clinging to the trunks.

Luckily, due to the high tide, we did not have far to wade. Suddenly, there above our heads was an untidy bundle of twigs and from it peered the fierce, yellow eye of a mottled, brown chick. Beyond, we could see similar nests, one in every treetop. Adults, grey and white with distinctive black caps and white plumes, circled overhead squawking at the intruders. Young Liam answered with a cheeky imitation from his safe perch on daddy's back. Rarely seen, black-crowned night herons hunt by night for fish in the brackish rivers further inland, retreating to their mangrove hideout to sleep and breed, producing sometimes three clutches a year.

The Chinese boatmen had obviously never seen the birds before or even suspected they existed within a few miles of their homes. We thought, as one of them spoke animatedly to Chong Peng, that they were quite interested in the heronry. It was only later that Chong Peng translated for us. The boatman had asked for permission to take a few of the birds home. They looked, he said, as if they would make good eating!

* * *

We swept up the broad driveway to the Taiping rest house. Coated with thick, dried mud we smelled as if we had just climbed out of the sewers but the girl behind the desk pretended not to notice and handed us our room key.

From here we telephoned the rest house in Grik at the western side of the new highway, for we planned to stay there the following night. After an hour of dialling we got through.

"Could we book a room?" we asked in Malay.

"Uh!"

We tried again in English; the response was the same.

We attempted once more in Malay. English. Malay again.

"Can you hear?"

"Uh!"

"We want to book a room for tomorrow night."

"Uh, uh!"

Did that mean yes? There was only one way to find out.

The road to Grik was a narrow one. Slim rubber trees arched over it, their nuts exploding with loud cracks in the heat and pelting our car. They stood in precisely spaced rows, corridors between the trunks opening up, perpendicular, diagonal, perpendicular, diagonal, like optical games, as we flashed past. We had at first vaguely thought of them as tin trees, standing to attention in toy soldier rows.

The trees opened out. A vista of the purest green stretched out to left and right. Nothing in this world, not emeralds or jade, nor even the Irish grass, approaches the vivid greenness of rice *padi* and greenest of all are the tiny, luminescent nursery patches which sprout in swampy corners. Small wooden houses perched among the fields sharing their islands with bending coconut palms. Earlier on in our journey we had seen freshly harvested *padi* fields, the farmers busy behind privy-like screens, thrashing their bundles, husks clouding the air around them. For the heat does not fluctuate and *padi* seasons can be dictated at will by the opening and closing of irrigation channels.

Grik. The name of this town is synonymous with exile, for it is to this outpost in the far north of Perak, near the Thai frontier, that government servants can be transferred as punishment for misbehaviour. It is also the dread of newly qualified teachers as it may take them years of repeated applications before they can return to 'civilisation'.

Rumah rehat. The signpost for the rest house pointed up a street prominently flanked with two no entry signs. We entered and made for a wooden building on a hill.

"We booked a room yesterday," we told the man at the desk hopefully.

He looked perplexed and checked his register. The rest house was already full.

His smooth brow puckered. He looked tired. "Who speak on telephone?"

"I'm not sure."

"Man or woman?"

"Well . . . eh . . . it was difficult to say." We dangled our baby urging him to produce one of his winning smiles.

The man ignored him and gazed along the verandah. "Maybe you stay in Sultan's room."

We looked at each other. "The Sultan?" we queried. Surely we would not be allowed to use the Sultan's room, that of Duli Yang Maha Mulia Paduka Seri Sultan Idris Almutawakkil Alallahi Shah Ibni Sultan Iskandar Shah Kadasallah DK, DMN, DK (Johore), DK (Pahang), SPCM, Sultan of Perak?

"I no give to Chinese or Indian," the man continued. He was a Malay. "They make very dirty. But Europeans . . . "

We wondered if he had noticed our lively and very destructive son.

He led us along the veranda to an open door. His wife was giving the room a final check, peering inside cupboards and under the bed. We stepped inside. The Sultan's room ! We laughed. Sultan! Stay here! The room was furnished in typical rest house style. Scuffed, ancient, wooden furniture filled the spacious room. Admittedly the royal colour dominated; indeed the greatest variety of yellow had been employed in the decor. The standard rattan set, its glass table top replaced with plywood, had long ago been painted a pale, insipid primrose. The worn seat covers clashed loudly in glaring saffron. Three threadbare rugs in mustard, gold and buff stretched to cover most of the linoleum on the floor. The curtains flaunted a pattern of orange squares. The table and dressing table had been neatly covered with lemon-coloured paper stapled down under sheets of plastic. The monstrous double bed, its head-board richly upholstered with teddy bear pelts, was spread with a fine coverlet of orange-embroidered, citron nylon. Above it a loose wire dangled nakedly, its function a mystery. Only in one corner, where a gaming table stood, was the harmony broken with fresh green baize. We opened the bathroom door. A broken pipe dripped vigorously and rust stained the bath. The drain was littered with cigarette butts. The plastic toilet brush was yellow.

There was a knock at the door. It was the manager. "If you find pistol and bullet, please to give me."

We gaped. A pistol! A bullet! In a country where illegal possession of a single bullet is enough to hang a man!

"The Sultan lose here yesterday," he explained and with an anxious look swept out. We gazed around the jaundiced room and pulled open a drawer. A pack of playing cards slithered forward. No pistol. No bullet.

The Sultan, it transpired, did use his rest house suite. He had in fact just left that morning after two nights of partying with two hundred guests.

A smooth-faced Chinese man told us about it. He had approached us with a greeting earlier, reminding us that we had met briefly on Pangkor Island a few weeks previously.

He indicated a heap of empty beer bottles. "No one could sleep. What a noise!"

"What were they doing," we asked.

"Oh, having fun, lah. Many people want to speak to the Sultan."

It was the Sultan's duty as Head of State of Perak to tour his domain, to become acquainted with the needs of his subjects. The rich and influential flocked for audiences and the Sultan showed no prejudice. Chinese, Malays and Indians could all approach him. Any willing to support the state economy were welcome as long as they knew where their first contribution should go. He had even turned down his chance of being King; as National Sovereign, he would have been too distracted to supervise the welfare of his own state.

Malaysia has a unique system of monarchy. There are seven Sultans, one Rajah and one Yang di-Pertuan Negeri, each of them rulers and Head of Islam in their own states. The office of Yang di-Pertuan Agong or King rotates among them, each new one being elected by the Council of Rulers to reign for five years at a time. Under a federal system of government, each of the eleven states in Peninsular Malaysia is administered not only by the Federal Parliament in Kuala Lumpur, but also by its own state government. Each Sultan is theoretically a figurehead and, although he is supposed to give his assent to bills passed by the state legislature, he has been known to refuse, especially if he doesn't see eye to eye with the state's Chief Minister or Mentri Besar.

A portrait of the Sultan gazed solemnly down at us from above the bar, his expansive white tunic splattered with medals, his chief wife, the Raja Permaisuri plumply filling the frame next to his. This Sultan had four wives and although the identity of his fourth changed from time to time, he kept to the number permitted by Islam.

The smooth-faced Chinese man gazed up at the portrait.

"How do you feel about the Sultan?" we asked.

He smiled gently. "Well . . . he is the Head of State in Perak."

He was obviously reluctant to say more. We changed the subject.

"What do you do?"

He worked for the LLN, the electricity board, and was in Grik for a week or two to check facilities.

We explained our presence in the country. He had a relative in our town.

"He is having a blue Renault, AX 612." We nodded and smiled vacantly. Considering his relative's identity established he turned his attention to food.

"Have you taken your *makan*?" he queried.

We hadn't. The rest house dining room was being used for an official function that evening. The Chinese man knew of a good *kedai* in town and suggested we eat together.

He hopped into our car and directed us down the hill into the town. New concrete buildings marked Grik's sudden rise to prominence, its position no longer at the end of the road but at the beginning of one — the new East-West Highway. A crowd gathered round a heap of durians being piled out of the back of a truck. Some of the squatting men wore cloths bound around their heads, loose ends trailing down the backs of their necks, a hint of the east coast.

"Can you take durians?" enquired our companion.

"Yes," we sighed. How many times had we been asked this question?

"And rice? Can you take rice?"

"Can," we groaned in unison and followed him into the *kedai*.

It was an Indian Muslim restaurant. At the door a dark, portly man twirled sheets of dough around his splayed fingers. The rubbery, white paste spread centrifugally until, just as it had reached a transparent thinness, he forestalled its ripping and slapped it on to a vast, oiled, hot plate. As it cooked he swiftly turned, folded and chopped it, and then deftly scooped the pieces on to a plate. We ordered some of these *roti chanai* which came with saucers of hot, thin *dahl*.

A television, perched high above the tables, commanded the attention of most of the customers. A sentimental American serial was coming to an end. Clear-skinned, clean-living kids crowded together smiling mistily for the tear-jerking finale. Immediately afterwards a documentary began. We could scarcely believe our eyes and ears. For half an hour of prime weekend viewing time, an ancient British film described to the inhabitants of this most tropical of countries, the intricacies of building a frost-proof, insulated chicken coop!

On our return to the rest house we peeped into the dining room. The long tables were lined with carefully mixed racial representatives, all men. Chinese, Malays and a few Indians sat stiffly and silently together in their batik shirts. Someone spoke and all those in the vicinity laughed loudly with relief and returned to self-conscious silence. A Chinese man produced a camera. Faces of every hue forced themselves into expressions of jollity. The shutter captured the occasion and impassiveness returned. Then the food arrived and the tension eased as rice was dished generously on to neighbour's plates and the obligatory halal chicken curry passed around.

"There are three races in Malaysia," our companion informed us.

We had noticed. Hastily we wished him good night and headed back to our yellow suite.

* * *

We left Grik early in the morning and had soon passed the check point. There were no villages or fields, no plantations or kampong houses along the road. The vegetation had been cleared on each side. It was an unusual Malaysian road for it had a vista and that vista was a magnificent one. Forested ribs of mountain ranges stretched in all directions, on the left into Thailand, on the right down the peninsula. The road had broken completely new ground. Clouds scudded overhead across a bright sky. Fresh breezes buffeted the car. We felt optimistic. We had expected a scarred landscape and although the road and its fringes showed as a fresh wound, it carried us aloft and presented us with immense views of primary forest.

We dipped down to cross a huge lake — the new Temenggor dam. Whitened tree skeletons poking above the surface indicated the drowned forest below. Then we were up again, sailing above the forests with the clouds. At regular intervals we could see clusters of huts perched on bluffs high above the road, and from sandbagged posts bored soldiers gazed over their machine guns. The remnants of the communist forces from time to time penetrate into Malaysian territory from their camps in the forests on the Thai side of the border and the new road, while linking the two coasts, also presents a barrier to their incursions.

Rain ambushed us as we reached Kota Bharu. Lightning exploded and rivers poured on to the car. The wipers oscillated frantically yet we could see nothing beyond the streaming water. We were trying to find the house of some friends, other teachers who had been posted to this town in the north-east. We could scarcely discern the road let alone the street names, few as they were. Two small boys on enormous bicycles appeared beside us, their white school shirts glued to their backs, their faces grinning with exhilaration. They laughed at the rain. They had nothing to lose. They could get no wetter. Their grins widened with added glee as they spotted our anxious, white faces peering through streaming windows.

"Mat Salleh, Mat Salleh," their cries went up. Their cheekiness delighted them.

The rain slackened. We sought informants. Did they know Lorong Haji Pak Noh, the street where our friends' house was. An impenetrable looking Chinese mechanic wasted little energy on facial expression. A slack-mouthed Malay boy in a roadside *kedai* looked at us with consternation. We turned up a side road and asked a woman standing at the porch of her house. She denied knowledge of the street. This was strange because she lived next to it and our friends were almost her next door neighbours.

The market in Kota Bharu captured us for most of the day. Here we discovered the east coast. The Chinese were scarcely to be seen; instead Malay women reigned, but of a different breed to their demure and retiring west coast sisters. Lengths of cloth swathed loosely and flamboyantly around their heads, they called to us as we passed, grinning provocatively with broken teeth, cheeky, brown eyes and wizened faces.

One suffocating corner of the market was tightly packed with material stalls draped with lengths of batik for which the east coast is famous. We bought several lengths of soft cotton densely patterned in blue and brown and brick red.

"Where is this from?" we asked as an afterthought. Perhaps it was from Kota Bharu itself or from Terengganu.

"Indonesia." The stall owner pointed to the gummed label.

The upper part of the market was quieter and crowded with piles of baskets, conical pandanus food covers in bright colours and designs, mats, hats and sieves, heavy brass Islamic metalwork and light, silver teapots with dense, embossed patterns. The women held out cracked, brown hands to take our smooth, white baby. Their laughter encouraged him to perform, smiling and clapping his hands, for Malays have a way with children; they cherish them above everything and baby boys are especially indulged and pampered. Ours was in danger of being thoroughly spoiled in the country.

As we left the market a taxi driver hailed us. "You go Rantau Panjang? You go Thailand?"

His collective taxi was half-full. We looked over. Two men stared back. We could guess their aim in visiting Thailand. From the border town of Rantau Panjang it is a brief trishaw ride to Sungai Golok and there pretty young girls, many of them teenagers, some lured from the villages of the north and unable to escape, fill the brothels while the pimps grow rich. But the traffic is not one way, syphilis and gonorrhoea accompany the men on their return trips ready to infect unsuspecting wives. Kota Bharu VD clinics do a brisk trade.

We headed south past fields of short, unattractive tobacco plants, a crop on the increase in the east but rarely seen in the west. We stopped at a petrol station. The girl attendants were all draped in *tudungs* — nuns brandishing petrol pumps, testing oil levels and cleaning windscreens.

A little further along the road we were amused to see an old man on a bicycle with a monkey perched patiently on the handlebars in front of him. He was on his way to his coconut plantation. There the monkey, a pig-tailed macaque and relative of the common long-tailed macaque, would save the old man a lot of work. Secured by a leash, it would clamber to the top of the trees and hurl down coconuts, having been trained to recognise exactly which ones were ripe.

We took a side road to Kuala Besut. We knew the teacher who had been posted there. His house was unusually easy to find, situated on a sandy track running parallel to the ocean. Scattered wooden kampong houses crouched among statuesque coconut groves.

Our friend was not at home, but we had expected this as it was holiday time. We rattled the little gate. A crowd of tousled children appeared to stare vacantly at us. To every question they responded "*Ta tahu* (don't know)." We left them scuffling aimlessly in the dust and walked towards the beach. The vast South China Sea stretched away before us. This was the east coast, symbol of rural Malaysia, the preserve of the Malays. A brisk breeze dishevelled the high fronds of the curving palms. Sun and wind conspired to bleach all noise from the scene. A dreamlike spell hung over the little house, the arching palms, the glaring sand. The place seemed timeless, detached from the world, existing in a bubble of windy deafness. Distant thunder rumbled as if through a barrier of cotton wool. Inland, the sky was leaden. Lightning flared but the sea was bright and the sun shone down hotly. The rain was elsewhere. Too noisy, too real, it had no place here. It could not break this coastal spell.

We untied the flimsy gate and climbed on to the veranda of the house. What was it like living here in the deafening silence? Idyllic or maddening? We could not reflect for long. Sandflies, though tiny and innocuous looking, inflict bites which take weeks to heal. One, two, a few and then dozens were upon us. We scribbled a note for our friend and rushed to the car.

There was a rest house in nearby Kampong Raja. We asked for directions. Hands waved in the air, fingers pointed skywards, rights and lefts were confused. It occurred to us that rural Malaysians, never having strayed far from their homes, had no idea what it was like to be on new territory and were thus incapable of giving coherent directions.

Early next morning a fisherman, who had heard of our interest in visiting Perhentian island, appeared at the door of our room and we arranged to make the trip with him. Perhentian is typical of the paradise isles of the east coast where coral flourishes in the unsilted waters. Although fishermen from a kampong on the nearby smaller island use the harbour, no one actually lives on Perhentian Besar. A few huts, however, are available for visitors and we established ourselves in one of these.

Little sandy coves backed by coconut groves bordered the island and for a few days we lived a desert island idyll, swimming in the clear, blue water, stalking the giant monitor lizards which left great web-footed tracks on the pale beaches and cooking fresh fish over a fire of coconut husks. The local fishermen visited us often. Dark, weather-beaten, piratical-looking men, they appeared fiercer and rougher than the more delicate mainland Malays but they were no less friendly and were ever eager to pick up our little blond baby and dandle him on their laps.

Every day we put on masks and snorkels and headed out to the coral reefs. The water was the clearest we had ever seen, so clear it was almost invisible. Below, different varieties of coral stretched in patterned formations, some parts like miniature, dense, conifer forests, others like curving fans, huge folded brains and stags' horns in subtle, pale blues and browns. Fish which roamed through these forests were more fantastic than those in the most imaginative and colourful child's picture book. Big parrot fish with blotches of blue, green and pink nibbled noisily at the coral with fat, purple lips. Yellow, white and black angel fish trailed long plumes behind them in the water. Oblong ones contoured with close yellow and purple stripes slunk among the coral while orange, white and black clown fish darted in and out of wavering anemone tentacles which would have killed any others but gave immunity to these little cleaners. Fish spotted like leopards lurked suspiciously in dark caverns along with puffy looking blow fish which, if caught, fill themselves so full of air they have difficulty sinking again if thrown back into the sea. Huge shoals of tiddlers flitted and swerved in tight formation, seeking safety in numbers. Occasional feeding turtles, perfectly camouflaged on the sea floor, sped off, startled by our approach. Among the rocks and coral the thick, wavy, coloured lips of giant clams opened and closed gently. A close examination of the coral surfaces revealed bright blue and orange anemones like tiny Christmas trees or bottle brushes which, when prodded, retreated into their holes. Now and then the evil, coral-consuming crown of thorns starfish could be seen, a current threat to the reefs although minor compared with the thoughtless dynamiting of fishermen intent on big catches but mindless of the permanent damage to their breeding grounds. Everywhere in Malaysia vast stretches of lifeless, grey coral can be seen, a result of this near-sighted greed.

The wonders of the coral reefs never ceased to fascinate us. There was always a new and fantastic fish or plant to be discovered and always a slight feeling of undefined dread of what might suddenly appear or what might be lurking, unseen. Sting rays and poisonous spiny fish were not uncommon and once in very shallow water a moray eel appeared from behind a rock, its ferocious jaws agape, like a mini Loch Ness monster. On another occasion, while snorkelling far from shore over deep water, we noticed a very large fish circling below us. We studied it for a while, marvelling at its size until it suddenly became apparent we were being watched by a shark. Speedily we flippered shorewards.

On our return to the mainland we jumped into the car and headed south, our goal the town of Kuala Terengganu and the house of some friends. Darkness soon fell but luckily rain didn't. Progress was hazardous enough. Although the main east coast road is a quiet country lane compared to the west coast suicide speedway, the local cattle and goats have not yet learned to avoid it. They wander across unconcerned about the swerving, screeching vehicles which not uncommonly collide with them. At night, we discovered, these animals pose an even greater hazard as they like to sit on the road to benefit from the stored-up heat.

Humans were also a danger after dark, when men in sarongs and *songkoks* gathered to exchange gossip, sitting on the edge of the tarmac, sauntering slowly to the mosque or wavering along the side of the unlit road on lampless bicycles. We were lucky not to hit anyone. Lights from approaching cars completely blinded us to these almost invisible cyclists. If ever we knocked one over, however, we had been advised not to stop but to drive straight to the next police station. We had heard too many stories of Malay villagers, their usual calm demeanour converted to rage, setting upon drivers who had stopped to aid accident victims, beating them and even throwing them into rivers.

During our days in Kuala Terengganu we made trips up the coast exploring the little kampongs dotted by the broad rivers and alongside the never-ending beach. Brightly painted high-prowed fishing boats were drawn up on the coarse sand facing the South China Sea. More than a shoreline, this coast is an integral part of the Malay consciousness. Although many originated from the west, from Indonesia, they look to the east as their source and as the heartland of their culture. Most Chinese bypassed this littoral on their way to the opportunities of the west coast and there were no plantations to draw the Indians. Even now most non-Malays shun the east where they see no place for themselves. It is here, the Malays believe, that the purity of their way of life is maintained and they see as evidence the traditional arts and crafts still being practised – the weaving of *songkets* and *pandanus* mats and the printing of batik. In the villages, top-spinning and kite-flying competitions are held and after the harvests ancient shadow puppet shows are sometimes performed. Imported with the early Malays from Indonesia, they relate the Hindu epic of the Ramayana, but their future, as the Malays redefine their identity as Muslims rather than South-East Asians, may be in jeopardy.

From the vast waters of the South China Sea the fishermen draw their livelihood although in December and January they must beach their boats as the monsoons arrive, inundating the coastal towns and villages. Also from this ocean when the seas are quiet come Vietnamese refugees (usually of Chinese extraction), those who have survived predatory Thai pirates and deprivations at sea in overcrowded and often sinking boats, arriving exhausted on the beaches to a reception that is far from friendly.

The same calm season brings other, much more welcome immigrants to these shores when female giant leatherback turtles heave their huge bodies up the steep, grainy beaches to lay their eggs. Round and white like ping-pong balls, these eggs are a sought-after delicacy and fetch a high price in local markets. This species of turtle would, in fact, be in great danger of extinction had not the government recognised the threat and posted officers along the laying beaches. Fishermen can collect the eggs, usually about one hundred per turtle, but fifty per cent must be given to the government hatcheries where they are guarded day and night until the babies emerge from their eggs, scrabble their way to the surface and make straight for the sea.

It is easy to watch these great animals laying their eggs. Many come ashore every night but we had heard terrible stories of mobs of onlookers tormenting the turtles, riding on their backs and kicking sand in their faces. It was not a sight we were keen to witness and the August school holiday is peak turtle-watching time. However we decided to give it a try and rented a little wooden hut for the night on the beach at Rantau Abang.

IM-I

At 3 a.m. the call went up — "Turtle!" Within minutes the quiet beach was mobbed as about 200 people appeared from nowhere and rushed for good positions. But there was no need to hurry. The huge turtle is a slow-moving creature on land and when we finally arrived, after a mile-long trudge along a moonless strand, it had only just finished excavating the hole for its eggs. The crowd was orderly and stood silently in darkness around the labouring creature, for the official egg collectors were adamant that there should be no lights. If a turtle is unduly disturbed at this stage it might return to the sea without laying. A deep, hoarse, gargling, aqualung breathing broke the silence and as we strained our eyes we could just make out the enormous rounded shape and the dim flashes of white as the eggs, caught one by one as they plopped from its body, were stowed in a sack.

Suddenly torches went on, cameras flashed and pandemonium reigned. The mob surged forward. Squeals of protest and curses in many languages broke the silence as two hundred people fought for photographic positions. The officials, uninterested in the turtle now its eggs had been safely laid and gathered, stood back. We retreated, our hearts sinking, Liam wailing. It seemed we were going to witness the scene we had hoped to avoid. But after the first excitement had passed and the essential photos had been snapped, the crowd thinned. We returned for another look. There, laboriously covering the pit and its non-existent eggs, we could clearly see, for the first time, this great turtle. Some six feet in length (they can grow to over eight feet), its shell was a dark, mottled green and from its eyes oozed jellylike 'tears', a mucous produced to keep sand from its eyes while ashore. Round and round it shuffled, pushing the sand behind it with its great flippers, floundering, apparently disorientated and unable to move its enormous weight back down the beach.

Then, eventually satisfied with its work, and having caught the scent of the sea, it faced the ocean. Wheezing like an exhausted Darth Vader, it headed purposefully and with surprising speed down the sandy slope. We had stationed ourselves at the edge of the surf and watched exhilarated as, only a few feet from us, the great creature reached the water and launched itself into the waves. Back, at last, after its long and hazardous ordeal, it reared up its head for a last gulp of air and plunged out of sight into the depths of the ocean from which it would not venture for another year.

* * *

Driving south from Kuala Terengganu, the sea was never far from the road but the scenery was surprisingly dull, dry and scrubby. Along the way we left the state of Terengganu and entered Pahang and on arrival in its capital, Kuantan, we immediately felt the proximity of the west. Chinese and Indians were to be seen again in numbers, and holidaymakers, who had travelled east from Kuala Lumpur by the old cross-country highway, thronged the beach hotels. Malaysians were very fond of telling us that Kuantan was "coming up" and indeed this town is growing fast, a result of the discovery and exploitation of oil reserves off the coast.

We did not linger here. We were keen to cover some distance now and spent most of the next two days driving — west along the highway and then south through the back roads, past the endless rubber plantations, the forested hillocks and the occasional Chinese towns.

Too tired to push on to Malacca, we stopped for the night in Bahau, a small town remarkable, to our minds for one feature. When darkness fell the sky grew dense with wheeling swallows as they converged on the town centre, ranging themselves in closely packed rows along every available wire and covering the trees as if with instant blossoms. The inhabitants were not in the least surprised. This happened every night, but we stood fascinated while electric lines sagged beneath the weight of thousands of twittering birds.

* * *

Malacca. The name of this town, for most Malaysians, means history. For while the rest of the peninsula was too impenetrably clad with forest to interest early settlers and traders, the port of Malacca proved irresistible. Established first as an offshoot of the Indonesian Hindu Kingdom of Sri Vijaya, its good defensible position, navigable river and supply of fresh water led it to grow quickly. It was through Malacca that Islam first reached the Malay community in the 15th century. By 1498 the power of its Sultans extended over much of the peninsula as well as areas of Sumatra; then in 1509 the Portuguese arrived, eager to find a base from which to control the seas and the all-important spice trade. Two years later they conquered the town and remained for 130 years until attacked and ousted by the Dutch. The importance of Malacca began to decline as the British opened up ports in Penang in 1786 and on Singapore island in 1819, so the Dutch ceded the town to the British in 1824. These were the major Crown Territories of Malaya.

It is evidence of this early history which attracts tourists to Malacca — the remains of the Portuguese fort and the famous pink-painted Dutch Staadhuys and church in the centre of the town. But for most Malaysians these remnants bear little relation to their own history. Neither the Dutch nor the Portuguese were very interested in the hinterland and it was the British, in more recent times who wrought most changes in the country. In any case, in a country of immigrants, very few can look to the peninsula at all for their roots. The Malaysian idea of history is a hazy one. '*Hari Ini Dalam Sejarah* (Today in History)', a television programme, epitomises the problem, for this short documentary, screened twice nightly in Malay and English, rarely goes further back in time than the Second World War in its search for material. A sense of history can be a vital block in the building of a national consciousness but, in order to include all Malaysians, only the most recent events can be drawn upon.

In Malacca we were like tourists. We visited the historic buildings, clambered around the fort, toured the museum and rested on benches outside the tourist office. We wandered into the narrow, but traffic-congested streets of Chinatown. Perhaps the best preserved in Malaysia, and certainly in better condition than those of Penang, the little townhouses were a delight. Although built in a row, facing the street, each was cut off from its neighbour by freshly whitewashed walls jutting out from the facade at either side, the cleanly swept porches protected above by protruding, old, red tiled roofs. Door and window shutters were immaculately lacquered in shiny brown and neatly painted with gold Chinese ideograms.

Children scuttled around the shop fronts and the clatter of mahjong tiles rang out from the open doors of the cramped houses. Two aged women, in baggy, black, silk trousers and blue shirts, long plaits dangling down their backs, stopped to gossip in the street outside the large, ornate Cheng Hoon temple, the oldest in Malaysia. A mere stone's throw down the street the muezzin called from an old crumbling brick tower, the minaret of a sparsely attended mosque while a few yards further on a single pair of sandals lay outside the door of a small Hindu temple, sandwiched between shophouses.

Malacca is the home of the oldest Chinese community in Malaysia. After a visit by Cheng Ho, an envoy of the Ming Emperor, in 1409, trade links were opened up between the two countries and the Malaccan Chinese can trace their residence in the country back several centuries. Although many of them speak Malay as their first language, these Babas and Nyonyas, as they are called, have traditionally taken a great pride in their identity. They have long sought, but never gained, *bumiputera* status and as time passes more and more of them are being assimilated into mainstream Chinese society.

In the evening we visited a temple dedicated to Cheng Ho. Nearby stood a well which for centuries was the only source of pure water for the regularly besieged inhabitants. Poisoned several times by wily enemies, it stands now muddy and neglected, a wishing well for passing tourists. Peering for a moment into the gloomy depths a movement caught our attention. The surface broke and a dark head appeared. Clinging to the inner edge of the well the man sorted through a handful of sand and gravel, picked out a few five- and ten-cent pieces, stowed them on a ledge and disappeared again beneath the surface. Up and down, up and down, the man dived and surfaced and the pile of coins on the ledge grew. We shouted down to him and kept up a sporadic conversation with him between dives. The effort was worth it, he assured us. An hour's search each week produced M$30 to

M$40. But . . . "*Sejuk* (cold)," he chattered and disappeared again beneath the murky waters.

Intrigued by stories of a Portuguese settlement to the south of Malacca, we drove there the next morning. We scanned the faces of the passers-by but although their race eluded us they were certainly not Caucasian. Noticing a little cafe we ducked inside and ordered some breakfast. We surveyed the other customers. Obviously a strong Goanese connection had added colour to their skin. An old man settled himself beside us and began to chat in passable English. We asked him if he spoke Portuguese.

"Of course," he exclaimed proudly. "But an old type of Portuguese. A person from Lisbon would not understand what we say. After all," he added, "we have been here since 1511."

He smirked proudly, his eyes invisible behind thick, smeared glasses. We examined him more closely for European features but found none.

He had read our minds. "Ah, but we live very near the equator," he pointed out. "We get dark from the sun. If we don't live near the equator we are white like you." He tapped his leathery yellow-brown chest.

We asked about his personal origins, hoping for a complicated history but he seemed to know little of his background. He was simply proud to be a member of the Portuguese community here. He looked more Malay than anything but he was a Christian.

"Yes, we are all Catholics here," he told us. "Chinese, Indians, Portuguese like me — all are Catholics."

"Are there any Dutch settlers in Malacca?" we asked. Since they had come later it was likely they too had left representatives behind.

"Dutch!" The old man bristled, misunderstanding the question. "Dutch! If any of these rascals come here we will most certainly chase them off!"

People passed on the street and dropped into the cafe. There was a strong sense of community. A Chinese woman who had served our coffee called greetings to friends outside. The language certainly didn't sound familiar. Yes, she replied to our queries, she too spoke Portuguese. She had moved to the settlement as a young child. She now spoke Mandarin with her husband, English with her two-year-old daughter and Portuguese with her customers. She also spoke some Malay. Her daughter too was growing up trilingual and would study in Malay at school.

Reluctantly we left the cafe. We had a long drive ahead of us as we planned to return home by the longer coastal route. Taking the minor roads we headed north. Delightful kampong houses with distinctive, low, sweeping roofs lined the roadside but we were soon enveloped in oil palm plantations. They covered acre after acre, mile after mile. Only at the resort town of Port Dickson did they give way, temporarily, to beach-side motels.

Carey island, a large flat piece of land severed from the mainland by only a river channel, was our next destination. We had heard that some Orang

Asli of the Mah Meri tribe lived there and that some of the families were highly skilled in the carving of masks.

Getting across to the island posed no problem. A little barge ferried us and our car across the channel but on the other side we were confronted by a barrier across the road. Beyond stretched yet more expanses of oil palm. We explained our mission to the security guard but he appeared unmoved. Apparently we needed permission from Harrisons and Crosfield, the company which owned the island, before we could go anywhere on it. We had not realised this. Crestfallen we tried to persuade him to let us through.

We asked if he knew of the woodcarvers and the whereabouts of their village. Yes, but it was difficult to find, he replied. With that the guard produced a piece of paper and pen and proceeded to draw us a map. This looked hopeful. He must have changed his mind. We felt cheered.

Handing us the map the man looked suddenly perplexed. "But how to go there?" he asked. "You do not have permission." With that he returned to his guardhouse.

Perhaps he had been waiting for some 'tea money' but eventually realising we were not going to go away, he relented and raised the barrier ushering us through.

His map was accurate. We bumped our way through the estate and at length found the village among some peripheral rubber trees. Inside the woodcarvers' house two brothers were sitting. Their faces were remarkable, high cheek bones, long hook noses and slightly slanted eyes combining to produce a mask-like quality. But these faces were not wooden and immobile. They smiled gently as we appeared and urged us to join them inside. Several carvings stood by the door, rounded, slightly grotesque but somehow friendly figures, fashioned from a beautiful red-brown wood. Perhaps the most remarkable was a seated animal which dangled a chain of interlocking bracelets from the long fingers of its upheld hand. Its head was turned to one side and a loose wooden ball could be seen between its grinning jaws.

The main interest for these carvers, however, was mask-making. One of the brothers was seated on the floor putting a polish on three which he had just completed — strange faces with thick eyebrows, squat noses and long curved chins. We asked the meaning of the figures and faces. We had read that the masks were employed by the Orang Asli *bomohs* to draw away evil spirits which caused illness, the mask being placed on the sufferer's face. But the carvers smiled and said there was no particular significance. They simply practised the traditional craft of their family and followed traditional designs, adding others of their own invention from time to time. They took us to a shed outside where a couple of women sat cooking on a wood fire. At one end were blocks of wood, roughly shaped and surrounded by a thick carpet of shavings. They used a local tree, they told us, the *nyireh batu* (*carapa obovata*). They liked its hard, red wood.

The Mah Meri belong, strangely, to the Senoi Orang Asli category who mostly inhabit the forests of the central peninsula. We spent an afternoon with these charming people, sitting in the shade of their workshop hut. Life was not too hard for them, they told us. Although the island forest was rapidly giving way to oil palm there was plenty of work to be had on the plantations. The carvers made enough from their craft, some items being sold in Kuala Lumpur while others were bought by the occasional visitors who, like ourselves, managed to make their way to the village.

The carvers were certainly the richest members of the community. Towards evening the local children collected around their house for they owned the only television and ran it from a generator in the backyard. The voltage was insufficient, however, and we left the audience squinting closely at a squashed miniature version of 'Popeye the Sailorman', a craze which had just hit Malaysia.

* * *

Next morning we set off again, negotiating the conurbation of Port Klang, and were once again deep in the monotonous gloom of oil palm plantations. The sudden hill of Kuala Selangor came as a pleasant surprise, its tall white lighthouse far from the sea. We found the rest house nearby and had lunch there admiring the magnificent setting. Below us the Selangor river meandered in deep curves through the dense, coastal mangrove fringe to the distant sea and in the trees around the hilltop park a band of silvered leaf monkeys leapt and scampered, the bright orange babies clinging to the chests of their mothers. We were now not far from home and decided to press on. Oil palm plantations finally gave way to tall, airy coconut groves around Sabak Bernam and then suddenly we were in Telok Intan and on familiar ground.

Our circuit complete, we turned into our kampong. A figure pedalled by, heading home after another long, hot day. It was the Indian ice cream seller. While we had covered perhaps a thousand miles around his country, he had been pedalling to and fro every day along the same route. He had probably never seen the east coast or Malacca. Quite possibly he had never even seen the sea. Like so many of the Malaysian poor his life was dictated by the seven-days-a-week pursuit of a very few dollars.

Our neighbours appeared from their houses, the children keen to greet their friend Liam. We were glad to be home again. We knew, however, that with our contracts coming to an end we had only a few more months to spend in Malaysia. The thought saddened us. The little concrete box in the kampong had been our first, and so far only, home together. So much had happened to us in the three years we had been there. Malaysia had brought us together as we discovered the country and explored its paradoxes.

It had been a simple and happy period in our lives. Nevertheless, we realised that if we renewed our contracts and stayed longer the eventual re-adaptation to western life would be ever more difficult. We had to go back. We did not want to end up feeling strangers in our native land.

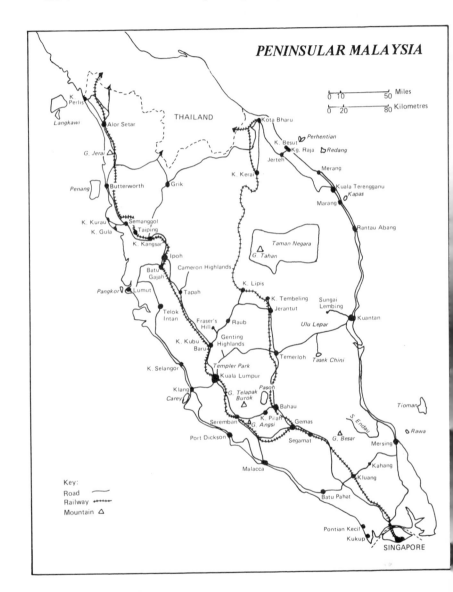

Appendix: Outstation

'Outstation' is a Malaysian English term for places out of the main cities. Since the sights of Kuala Lumpur, Penang and Malacca are well documented elsewhere and much useful information is available from tourist offices in these towns, we have chosen not to repeat it all but instead to concentrate on outstation spots which particularly appealed to us. Some are popular tourist areas, others are off the beaten track but well worth the effort necessary to reach them.

Accommodation: Rather than giving long lists of accommodation we provide, if applicable, details and telephone numbers of local government rest houses. Built by the British, primarily as temporary accommodation for government officials who went outstation on business, they occupy prime sites in most of the small to medium-sized towns. Most retain their colonial character with creaking wooden floors, ancient capacious rooms, enormous outmoded furniture and wide, breezy, scenic verandas. They are also reasonably priced and we stayed in them when we could. We mention those places where we found advance booking necessary at weekends and during school holidays.

Apart from rest houses, most places have a number of basic Chinese hotels which, however, tend to be a bit noisy. For those who have just arrived in the country and may be baffled by the bathroom arrangements, the big tub of water (*mandi*) is not a bath; you are meant to use the little plastic bucket to scoop water from it over yourself, filling it from the tap as necessary.

Public transport: There are frequent, hair-raisingly fast express bus services between major towns although if you want to go to a smaller place *en route* you may have to pay the full fare. Shared outstation taxis are almost as cheap (fares are standard) and depart from the ranks as soon as they have four passengers. This can sometimes mean a long delay while waiting for the full complement unless you are prepared to pay a bit extra to leave earlier. They can be a very convenient way to travel and will generally take you to your destination or the appropriate taxi rank for the next leg of your journey. Hitch-hiking is fairly easy and safe for westerners.

Natural history: In our descriptions of favourite places we emphasise the wildlife and, in particular the bird life. We do not attempt a comprehensive

127

guide so an interested reader may find the books mentioned in the 'Further Reading' section useful. For those with a keen interest in the natural world another valuable source of information is the Malayan Nature Society, PO Box 10750, Kuala Lumpur which has its office at 17 Jalan 2/53, Petaling Jaya, Selangor, Malaysia (tel: 03-753330). The Society has various branches all over the country and publishes two quarterly journals. Recently they have been composing a *Directory of Nature Recreation Areas in Peninsular Malaysia and Singapore* which, when complete, will be issued as a separate publication full of information on out-of-the-way spots for the nature lover.

We begin our guide in the south-west of the peninsula, work our way north along the west coast then from north to south along the east coast. Two additional sections fill in the details of the inland areas under the headings of 'Forest' and 'Hill Stations'.

Finally, throughout this appendix we tend to use the Malay terms for river etc. so a brief glossary of the most important terms may be useful. Thus *sungai* means river, *pulau*: island, *gunung*: mountain, *bukit*: hill, *pantai*: beach, *tasek*: lake and *kampong* (*kg*): village.

THE WEST COAST

The west coast is much more populated, developed and racially diverse than the east coast. Many visitors find it less interesting, or at any rate, not as charming. In fact there are many areas of interest but they must be sought out. We describe some of the more obscure of these.

The South-West: In the south-west of the peninsula, not far from the Singapore border, the little stilted fishing village of Kukup is famous for its sea food restaurants perched above the water. There are pleasant rest houses in Pontian Kecil, a little to the north, and in Batu Pahat (tel: 07-441181).

The next major point of interest in this coast is Malacca. The tourist office in the centre of the old town, has abundant information which we need not repeat. Look out in this area for the particularly lovely traditional architecture of the kampong houses with curving gables sometimes compared with cow-horns.

North of Malacca the oil palm plantations dominate the roadside until the beaches of Port Dickson break the monotony. This is a favourite resort for Kuala Lumpur residents, so numerous hotels and bungalows line the beach. It can make a pleasant break from the city but there are better beaches on Pangkor and Langkawi islands to the north.

Carey Island: Carey Island is separated from the mainland of Selangor only by the Sungai Langat. The island, which is privately owned by the Harrisons and Crosfield company, is almost entirely covered in oil palm. What makes it worth visiting are the Mah Meri Orang Asli a few of whom do exceptionally beautiful woodcarvings.

Carey Island can be reached from the south by turning left not long after Jugra, the hill which acts as a landmark in the district of Kuala Langat. Alternatively it is clearly signposted to the west several miles south of Port Klang on the road to Port Dickson. The river is easily crossed in a small antiquated ferry boat. Since the island is private property written permission to enter it should be obtained either from the Department of Orang Asli Affairs in Kuala Lumpur or from the manager of Harrisons and Crosfield on Carey Island. This is not always insisted on.

The Mah Meri village, Kampong Orang Asli, is at Sungai Bumbun about eight miles (13 kilometres) from the entrance. Drive as far as the roundabout and then take a left turn. Plantation workers are helpful if you get lost. Ask for Belon Kasim, one of the woodcarving brothers, and give yourself plenty of time to spend with these charming people. Not many outsiders make it to the village so they welcome visitors warmly.

If you are unable to visit Carey Island, a few Orang Asli woodcarvings can be found in the Karyaneka craft complex in Kuala Lumpur and a large number are sold in a little shop 11 miles (18 kilometres) from Kuala Lumpur on the old road to Pahang state near the Mimaland recreation centre and just before the Orang Asli hospital. (The shop is closed on Fridays.)

Kuala Selangor: The average visitor to Malaysia takes the main trunk road when travelling north or south from Kuala Lumpur or Penang and thereby misses Kuala Selangor Hill, a granite outcrop which rises prominently above the surrounding coastal plain. There are huge rain and fig trees which attract resident and migrant birds. There are several troops of monkeys, both long-tailed macaques and the relatively uncommon but here very tame, silvered leaf monkeys. The Kuala Selangor rest house at the top of the hill is a great place to stay although there are also hotels in the town of Kuala Selangor itself at the foot of the hill.

Coming from Kuala Lumpur there are two ways to approach Kuala Selangor: by travelling via Klang and up the coast or inland via Sungai Buloh through more pleasant countryside. It can also be reached from Telok Anson (now Telok Intan) in the north. The public bus will take you to Sabak Bernam and from there on to Kuala Selangor.

Kampong Kuantan: About six miles (10 kilometres) from Kuala Selangor the mangroves at Kampong Kuantan are famous for their flashing fireflies which 'perform' nightly in their thousands. A villager of Kampong Kuantan, Encik Jalaluddin, takes visitors out by boat, four or five at a time. He can be contacted at the general store, Kedai Eng Joo Huat, at the T-junction in Kampong Kuantan, usually between 7.00 and 7.30 p.m. Wear insect-proof clothes and shoes suitable for muddy paths.

Pangkor Island: One of the few idyllic islands off the west coast, Pangkor is connected by ferry from Lumut, a small town which is easily reached by bus or car in one and a half hours from Ipoh or Taiping. Coming from the south, Lumut can be approached via Telok Intan. The stretch of road after Kampong Gajah, on this route, is extremely picturesque and to our minds one of the most scenic in Malaysia. Wooden kampong houses nestle among tall durian and other fruit trees, opening out occasionally into smallish areas of lush *padi*. Stork-billed kingfishers as well as the common white-breasted kingfisher can be seen on wires above the *padi* fields. Look out also for black-shouldered kites on perches in open spaces or hovering above the fields. These birds are the farmers' friends, gobbling up pesky rodents which would otherwise destroy the *padi* crop.

In Lumut it is possible to stay in the very pleasant rest house (tel: 05-935938) just a stone's throw from the harbour. The main ferries run every half hour to the two Chinese fishing villages on the east coast of the island, a trip of between 35 and 40 minutes. The first, or more northerly, of the two villages is called Kampong Sungai Pinang Kecil (or Kg Sungai for short) and the second simply Kampong Pangkor. The latter has one reasonably cheap hotel – the Min Lian. Most people, however, take one of the few taxis or walk the one and a half miles (two kilometres) to the west side of the island which has most of Pangkor's tourist facilities. Here there are a few quite comfortable and not too expensive hotels. There is also a dilapidated and rather dirty government rest house. Slightly to the north is the cheap Mini Camp, popular with groups of Malaysian teenagers but unfortunately rather noisy and messy. The beaches on this part of the west coast have a very steep incline.

By staying at the hotel in Kampong Pangkor it is possible to avoid the drawbacks of the popular west coast and soak up some of the authentic local atmosphere and smelly charm of the stilted houses which overhang the sea. From there it is not too far to walk south through the lovely Malay kampongs to the remains of the Dutch fort built at least 300 years ago in order to control access to the Malayan mainland. Indeed, Pangkor has always been at the centre of Malaysian history and it was here in 1874 that the Treaty of Pangkor was signed establishing the system of so-called Residents in certain states of the peninsula for the first time and thereby passing economic control to the British.

There is another, smaller ferry boat which leaves from Lumut for Pangkor

Island but this one goes only to the Pangkor Bay Village Hotel at the northern neck of the island. Ferries leave four times daily at 8.30, 10.30, 13.30 and 16.15 from Lumut and return at 9.30, 12.30, 15.30 and 17.00 from Pangkor. The first ferry of the morning and the last of the afternoon connect with the main ferry at Kg Sungai and take about one hour. Otherwise it is a direct 40 minute trip to the lovely Oyster Bay on the north-east side of the island. From there a tractor/trailer takes Pangkor Bay Village guests on a five-minute trip to the hotel on the other side of the island.

The hotel consists mainly of chalets dotted around under coconut trees a few yards from a long, flat clean beach. There are wind-surfing and boating facilities available and the thick primary forest surrounding the bay is full of wildlife. Hornbills are abundant and sea eagles and brahminy kites can be seen wheeling overhead. At dusk colugos, the mis-named flying lemurs of S. E. Asia, glide between the coconut palms.

Bookings can be made at Ipoh Gardens Bhd, 41 Jalan Tasek, Ipoh Gardens South, Ipoh (tel: 05-557627/557709) or at the little office beside the ferry in Lumut. (It is advisable to book well in advance for holiday periods.) Pangkor Bay Village is expensive but you can stay in Lumut or at the Hotel Min Lian in Kg Pangkor and commute on the morning and evening ferries. (As the land at Pangkor Bay Village is privately owned day trippers may be charged a small fee.)

No roads connect the northern head of Pangkor to the rest of the island but there are paths on the east and west sides which are worth exploring. There is a small Malay kampong at Oyster Bay and from there it is just over two miles (three kilometres) through the forest to Kg Sungai. Try to do this walk at dawn.

If you are walking down the west side of the island you must again start from the Malay kampong in Oyster Bay but this time take the path to the west and cross over the neck of the island. In the early morning and the evening look out for wrinkled and great hornbills, white-rumped shamas, dollarbirds, great slaty woodpeckers and perhaps an Asian paradise fly-catcher. Long-tailed macaques are quite commonly seen next to the path.

Coral Bay is the first bay you reach although most of the coral is poor, as is usually the case wherever it is found on the west coast of Malaysia. Nevertheless, this is a beautiful, deserted bay with a gently sloping beach and overhanging trees. Just beyond Coral Bay lies Thomson Bay which has a small area suitable for camping, under tree cover at its northern end. (Bring all your food and drink with you.) The trees behind this beach are a favourite gathering site for large groups of cackling pied hornbills. From here it is a good hour's walk to the Mini Camp and the hotels or about 40 minutes back to Pangkor Bay Village.

It is possible to follow an old track behind Coral Bay across to Kg Sungai. The path twists and climbs over the top of the island (about 3,000 feet or

912 metres) on its way to the village. It is a deceptively long distance so do not make our mistake of bringing insufficient water and certainly do not try to regain Oyster Bay by attempting to come back through the heart of the forest.

Finally, it is worth renting a fishing boat from near the island's rest house and going to the smaller adjacent island of Pangkor Laut. You can spend the whole day or a day and a night on Emerald Bay and get the boatmen to come back and pick you up.

Pulau Sembilan: Pulau Sembilan means nine islands in English and it is possible to camp on at least two of them. These uninhabited islands are situated to the south of Pangkor and can be reached by a two- to three-hour trip on a fishing boat from Lumut. It is much better to do this with a large group since it may cost M$200 (US$80) to rent the boat. The two principal camping islands have running stream water and magnificent beaches. They are full of pied imperial pigeons which don't appear on Pangkor or the mainland. Bring all your food and drink and also a blanket and mosquito coils or you'll have a sleepless night. Although the coral isn't great bring your snorkel and mask. When you return with your rubbish don't give it to the boatman or you may find he empties all of it straight into the sea!

Kellie's Castle: This dilapidated but eccentric structure, described in the last chapter, is near Ipoh. About ten miles (16 kilometres) before Ipoh on the main road from Kuala Lumpur, turn left for the town of Batu Gajah. About three miles (five kilometres) before Batu Gajah the castle can be seen on the left-hand side on top of a rise across a small river.

There used to be a bridge over the river in the days when it was popular to visit the castle. It has, however, since disintegrated and visitors are rarities. To reach the castle now you must take off your shoes and wade across the river. The alternative would be a long hike through a rubber estate from much nearer to Batu Gajah. Don't try to approach through the small works yard as the proprietor doesn't welcome visitors. Instead cross at the buffalo ford a little upstream.

Ipoh: The Station Hotel (tel: 05-512588), if you can afford it, is the place to stay in Ipoh for a decaying breath of colonial Malaya in rooms big enough for a battalion. The town itself is functional and not very interesting except for some Chinese cave temples situated in the dramatic limestone outcrops both to the north and south of the town, just by the main trunk road. Those to the north, Perak Tong, house an enormous Buddha statue and many colourful murals; those to the south, Sam Poh Tong, feature a pond crammed with turtles, the Chinese symbol of longevity. Stalls to the south of the town sell the speciality of the area — great greenish-yellow pomelos, rather like large sweet grapefruit.

Kuala Kangsar and Taiping: Kuala Kangsar and Taiping are all too easily overlooked as places to visit simply because the main western trunk road bypasses the towns. Both, however, deserve a visit, the former for its elaborate old wooden Istana (palace) and the fine Ubadiah mosque, as well as the Malay College residential school. There is a quiet rest house (tel: 05-851699) overlooking the river.

Taiping has lovely lake gardens and is surrounded by mountainous rainforest, which also makes it the wettest place in Malaysia. It is from Taiping that Malaysia's oldest hill station, Maxwell Hill, is reached. (For further information see under Hill Stations section.) The rest house (tel: 05-823746), a rather soullessly modern but comfortable one, overlooks the lake gardens.

Both towns have stations on the western rail line and the train on the single track railway, especially between Kuala Kangsar and Taiping over Bukit Berapit, chugs its way through secondary forest with bamboos and ferns brushing against the train windows. Buses are frequent to both towns.

Kuala Gula: Kuala Gula is a small fishing village situated at the delta of the Sungai Selinsing in north-west Perak state. It is of interest because it is near to a sanctuary for the only Malaysian colony of the threatened black-crowned night heron.

Getting there without a car is unfortunately a little difficult. The drive to Semanggol, about 15 miles (24 kilometres) north-west of Taiping, is straightforward by bus or car. Thereafter follow the narrow western road towards Kuala Kurau. Those without cars should be able to hitch a lift on an oil palm lorry. After about ten miles (16 kilometres), a small unsignposted road goes off to the left. It is only two or three miles (about four kilometres) to Kuala Gula from that point although it can seem like an eternity due to the appalling condition of the road. The traveller without transport might have to walk this remaining distance.

It is advisable to try to arrange the trip well in advance at the Department of Wildlife and National Parks in Kuala Lumpur. (For details see the 'Forest' section.) If the rangers have advance warning of your arrival they should have sufficient supplies of petrol for the official boat. Otherwise, if you just turn up as we did, you may be able to hire a boat at the Chinese fishing village (we paid M$100 (US$40) for about three hours) but your trip depends on the willingness of one of the rangers to accompany you. This is especially unlikely outside office hours. Try to plan your trip to coincide with the highest possible tide as this will allow you to get close to the birds before getting out of the boat. You'll still have to wade some distance so wear an old pair of shoes.

It is a lengthy journey to the heronry because, since the sanctuary was started, the herons have moved further north in search of suitable mangrove for nesting. However, herons are not the only birds of interest to be seen at

Kuala Gula. It is also the only area where significant numbers of lesser adjutant storks and milky storks as well as five species of white egret can be seen. It is a magnificent trip and well worth the hassle.

Gunung Jerai (Kedah Peak): Gunung Jerai at 3,992 feet (1,217 metres) stands alone in the state of Kedah, north-east of Penang. The view from the top is magnificent — dawn over the Kedah plain and sunset over the Straits of Malacca. There are forest paths and a waterfall. Look out near the summit for bright mauve sonerila flowers which grow nowhere else but on this mountain. There is a well-established mountain track as well as a narrow, winding one-way road for the less energetic. To get there, turn off the main north-south trunk road near the town of Guar Chempedak. Those travelling by bus could ask to be let off at the Gunung Jerai junction and then walk to the foot of the mountain. You can spend the night near the top at a small rest house which can be booked in the government offices of Sungai Petani or Alor Setar.

Langkawi: Lying off the coast of Perlis, the Langkawi islands — 99 of them altogether — are a major attraction of the west coast. Until recently they were relatively untouched but the Malaysian government has grandiose plans to turn them into a major resort with enormous hotels, golf courses, a duty-free shopping centre, etc. How much of this 'dream' will come true remains to be seen but it is likely that the islands will be altered to some extent.

There are daily flights from Penang, Kuala Lumpur and Alor Setar. Otherwise the Ebban Express bus company runs a daily service from Butterworth to link up with the ferry. Boats usually leave three times a day — early morning, mid-morning and lunch time. It's advisable to get there by midday at the latest as times can vary.

There is accommodation in or near the main town of Kuah — a few small Chinese hotels in town, an expensive and rather plastic Country Club (with swimming pool) one and a half miles (two kilometres) from town and a rest house (tel: 04-749234) overlooking the bay at the edge of town. Accommodation can be difficult to find during the holiday seasons.

Kuah, though by the sea, does not have a beach. One way to reach the beaches and see the rest of the island is to hire a motorbike — but be careful to cover up exposed skin as you can get very burnt without realising it. You can also hire cars or bicycles or use local buses. Tanjong Rhu is a quiet beach on the north coast by a lagoon with shady casuarina trees, although government plans for tourist development are most likely to change this part of the island. Also on the north coast is Pasir Hitam, a black sand beach (too shallow for swimming) and on the west coast there are two extensive but unshaded beaches, Pantai Tengah and Pantai Cenang. (You may find, as we did, the sudden appearance of large numbers of curious locals a bit off-putting.)

There are plenty of places to visit apart from the beaches. From the village of Kuala Teriang you can hire a fishing boat to Pantai Kok, and from here trek through the forest for 45 minutes to Telaga Tujuh Waterfall which cascades down through a series of seven pools.

A highlight for most people is a trip to the second biggest island of Pulau Dayang Bunting with its large and exquisitely beautiful Lake of the Pregnant Maiden. It is believed that a drink of the water will cure infertility and many Malaysian women make the trip for this reason. The lake is deep but a wonderful place for swimming.

We went to the island with a party of Malaysians. Our trip included, to our mystification, a stop at a small pebble beach. Our fellow trippers leapt out of the boat with great glee and began collecting bagfuls of them. We later realised that this was because pebbles are rare in Malaysia. Boatmen will also, if asked, bring you to areas of coral. The best is between the islands of Beras Basah and Singa Besar. They can also bring you to good fishing areas. Look out for the 'Boat for Hire' sign in Kuah — they leave from the rickety jetty behind the shops — or ask at the hotels to find parties to join up with.

Langkawi is a prime spot for rare butterflies, although their habitats are being rapidly destroyed. Large monitor lizards frequent the beaches and there are plenty of pied hornbills and noisy hill mynahs. There are also chances to see some species of birds found only in the north of the country and in Thailand, for example the chestnut-headed bee-eater.

EAST COAST

Unlike the west coast, the east coast comprises almost unbroken beach. Another difference is its predominantly Malay population and slower, more rural, way of life. Since the population is overwhelmingly Muslim, and fundamentalism is taking a strong hold, it is advisable for tourists to dress modestly. From the practical point of view bear in mind that during the rainy season, from November to January, flooding can be so bad as to completely cut off the east coast states and cause evacuation of villages. The sea is also extremely rough at this time and it is either impossible or very difficult to get to any of the islands. The best part of the year, when the sea is at its clearest for snorkelling, is April to September.

It is also useful to remember that the states of Kelantan and Terengganu, together with Kedah and Perlis in the north-west, have their weekend on Friday and Saturday.

IM–J

The North-East: In the north-east of the peninsula, not far from Thailand, lies one of the main east coast towns, Kota Bharu. The town is rapidly modernising but the market, near the centre, remains little changed and is worth a wander, especially upstairs in the quieter and friendly basket and metalwork area. Kota Bharu is also the easiest place to come across traditional pastimes such as top-spinning, drumming, dancing and shadow puppet shows. Check the tourist office for times and venues. You may also see bird-singing contests held at dawn on Friday mornings. Cages of peaceful doves (*merbok*) are hoisted up on 25-foot (9-metre) poles and judged for the quality of their soft, melodious trilling. A major competition is held in June. There are many handicraft factories — woodcarving on Jalan Pengkalan Chepa, silverware in Kg Sireh off Jalan Sultana Zainab and kite-making and batik on the road to the Beach of Passionate Love (Pantai Berahi).

In reality this somewhat inappropriately named beach is a rather average one, and curious small boys would certainly prevent the passions from becoming inflamed. Better beaches are Pantai Desar at Sabak, an eight mile (13 kilometre) bus ride to the north or at Bachok, about a 12 mile (20 kilometre) shared taxi ride to the south. The best one of all, with white sand and shady casuarina trees, is Pantai Dalam Rhu, 30 miles (48 kilometres) to the south, near Semerak.

Perhentian Island: One of the highlights of a visit to the east coast can be a trip to one or more of the offshore islands. Perhentian is not especially easy to reach but well worth the effort. People will tell you that boats leave for Perhentian from Kuala Besut. This is true. However, the only place to stay in the area is the rest house at Kg Raja, across the river, and as boats leave early in the morning you will probably need to spend a night there. A ferry carries foot passengers across the river but if you approach by car, be sure to drive directly to Kg Raja (turn off main road at Jerteh). The rest house, despite its pleasant position by the beach, is notorious for its dirty rooms, slovenly service and atrocious food. Grin and bear it. If you ask around, (and you may have to cross on the ferry to Kuala Besut), one of the fishermen will offer to take you out to the islands and possibly collect you from the rest house beach. The trip will cost at least M$50 (US$20) and takes about two hours. The boatman will wait to take you back if you go for the day, otherwise make arrangements for your return trip. As on all boat trips, protect yourself well from the sun. An umbrella is useful and don't forget to cover your feet.

There is a rest house on the island of Perhentian Besar, a collection of three basic huts with bathrooms. They are quite popular and must be booked at the Kg Raja district office beforehand. (It closes about 4 p.m.) You will need to take all your own food although you can get fish from the fishermen (who live on Perhentian Kecil but fish from Perhentian Besar) and you can cook on coconut husk fires. There is tap water in the rest house huts. Around the coast a little, there is a collection of huts for rent from the headman (who doesn't speak English), Mat Sidik b. Batin Talib PJK. His address is Wakil Pos, Pulau Perhentian, Kelantan. You can also camp. There is beautiful coral, particularly if you walk about two beaches from the rest house huts. Take care not to get your back burnt while engrossed in underwater wonders; wear a T-shirt.

Kuala Terengganu: Kuala Terengganu is similar to Kota Bharu with an equally pleasant market. You can take boats to the various islands in the estuary and visit the boat-building yards. The road approaching Kuala Terengganu from Kota Bharu takes an inland route but it is well worth following the coastal road north through typical east coast palm tree grove kampongs, past the fishing village of Batu Rakit to Merang. From where the road ends at a wonderfully positioned ruined house, you can walk along the beach between the lagoon and the sea. It is quiet and very atmospheric, especially if there is a storm approaching.

Other interesting excursions are possible if you follow roads beside the river and its tributaries. The more intrepid can trek into the forested areas inland from Kuala Terengganu. It is, theoretically, even possible to walk into Taman Negara, the national park. For any such expeditions guides are essential but local villagers, who go into the forest regularly and know it well, can be hired. In early 1984 there were two reported sightings in Kelantan of the extremely rare Javan rhinoceros (previously considered extinct in the peninsula and down to the last 55 in Java) so you could have a very exciting trip.

Several very beautiful islands are accessible from Kuala Terengganu or from Marang to the south. Pulau Kapas is the nearest and best suited to a day trip as it is only half an hour from Marang (not to be confused with Merang). The water is clear and the coral good. Much further out to sea are the nine islands of the Redang Archipelago. It can take between three and five hours to get to Pulau Redang, the largest island and also the only inhabited one. (On the way, look out for Pulau Bidong Laut, used as a transit camp for Vietnamese refugees.) The coral, particularly off the west coast of Redang, at Pasir Macham Ayam, is some of the best in Malaysia. In addition, four species of turtle lay their eggs along the north-west coast. So good is the coral here it is hoped that the peninsula's first National Marine Park may be established around Redang. Bring food supplies and be prepared to camp on the beach.

Turtles: One of the chief attractions of the east coast for foreign and Malaysian tourists alike, are the giant leatherback turtles which lay their eggs from May to September on the stretch of beach between points to the south of Kuala Terengganu and the north of Kuantan. As we have described, it can be a jostle and nature lovers may decide to forego the experience. The prime laying area is at Rantau Abang. Here you can either stay in the cheap but basic and rather noisy chalets on the beach or the more plush Visitors Centre with its award-winning, traditionally designed, turtle museum nearby. You will be awakened at either place by the turtle alert service and at least one turtle comes in every night during the August peak season. Alternatively, if you want to find a turtle all of your own you can walk far up the beach, even camping for a few nights, and you may be lucky.

Further south, towards Kuantan, there are a number of motels with laying beaches, although turtles are not so plentiful or regular here. We found the Chendor Motel (tel: 095-31369) pleasant enough. There is an interesting scrub area close by with civet cats, monitor lizards and pied hornbills. On the beach just in front of the Motel is a fenced-in area used for the hatching of turtle eggs. Each group of eggs is marked with the date of laying. Fifty-four days later the little babies emerge from the sand and make for the sea. This is fun to watch. No matter how you point the babies, they somehow know exactly where the sea is and scuttle towards it as fast as they can.

Around Kuantan: The most popular place to stay in Kuantan is by the beach at Telok Chempedak, four miles (six kilometres) from town. There is a modern, but heavily booked, rest house known as the Annexe (tel: 095-21043) and there are plenty of cheapish hotels in the area.

Fifteen miles (24 kilometres) outside Kuantan, a Buddhist monk once made himself at home in the Panching caves and constructed temples and a reclining Buddha. To reach the caves, take the road towards Sungai Lembing and turn right near the 15 milestone (24 kilometre) point. Continue through plantations until you reach the rock face and be prepared to clamber up steep steps to the cave network.

Further from Kuantan, off the main Kuantan-Temerloh road, there are two places of interest. The first is a lake, Tasek Chini, situated to the south of the road. Thirty-five miles (56 kilometres) from Kuantan, take the road to the left and continue for about 15 miles (24 kilometres) to Kg Chini. Here boats can be hired to go through the reedy inlets to the lake. Look out for the Malaysian equivalent of the Loch Ness monster which is believed to lurk there.

From about the same point on the Kuantan-Temerloh road you can turn north to reach the forested area of Ulu Lepar. For directions see the 'Forest' section.

Tioman Island: South of Kuantan the largest and most popular east coast island, Tioman, lies 35 miles (56 kilometres) off the town of Mersing in Johore. This picturesque island is mountainous and forested in the centre, with sandy beaches and excellent coral mainly on the west coast. Boats leave from Mersing. Go to the tourist office near the harbour where local boatmen hang around to offer their services. Alternatively try to get on the faster and much more comfortable Merlin Hotel boat even if you are not staying there. Fishing boats take about three to four hours and leave according to the tides. Look out for Christmas frigate birds with their deeply forked tails and for dolphins coming alongside the boat to have a look. If you should need to stay in Mersing overnight there is a good modern rest house (tel: 07-791101) overlooking the sea.

Tioman (scene of *South Pacific*'s Bali Hai) is becoming popular with young travellers and the amount of cheap accommodation is growing. We liked Roger's beach-side rooms. There is also a dormitory behind the Merlin and a very basic rest house. A man called Nadzri has bits and pieces of accommodation all over the place including some at the quiet Monkey Bay, some distance from the main jetty and village.

Snorkelling is best right in front of the Merlin. Look out for turtles and for small sharks in deeper water. Look out also for flying lizards among the coconut trees. A forested path, starting behind the airstrip, takes you across the island. It involves quite a sweaty climb but there is a very refreshing waterfall near the top. On the other side there is a little harbour and restaurant where you can stay for the night. Beware of the sandflies on the beach here. You won't notice them biting but the lumps they leave are fearsomely itchy and remain for weeks.

Several other much smaller islands, closer to the coast and also accessible from Mersing, are being developed for tourists. Pulau Rawa is the chief one of these with white sand beaches and bungalows. Another is Pulau Babi Besar. Enquire at the tourist office for further information.

Train journey across the peninsula: For those who have travelled north along the east coast and would like to return by an alternative route it is possible to take the train and, by prior arrangement, possible even to put a car on it. Although we never did it, the journey, which snakes through the heart of the country, is supposedly an interesting one for all rail enthusiasts. The stretch from Kuala Kerai in Kelantan to Kuala Lipis in Pahang is the wildest and the single track railway passes through some of the remotest kampongs in Malaysia. It is, however, a very long journey and the train has to take a circuitous trip south to Gemas before heading north again to Kuala Lumpur. For details enquire at Malayan Railways in Kuala Lumpur.

FOREST

This section deals primarily with relatively undisturbed forest, a swiftly diminishing part of Malaysia. In general it is difficult to get to true primary rainforest but we describe how to find a few of the more accessible areas as well as suggesting trips to remoter regions.

When jungle trekking don't leave the path as you quickly lose your bearings. Carry a compass if you make any extensive treks. Never camp right next to rivers or on islands as the level can rise dramatically overnight. Probably a hammock, with a groundsheet slung across branches to keep off rain, is the best sleeping arrangement. Leeches can appear in hordes especially after wet weather but the best preparation is a philosophical attitude. Some recommend tightly tied boots with trousers tucked into socks which have been pre-soaked in salted water or insect repellent; others claim it is better to wear shorts so you can see them more easily. In fact leeches will get you anyway but apart from producing a lot of annoying gore they don't do much harm. To get them off, the touch of a lighted cigarette or match or a drop of salt usually does the trick.

Templer Park: This park is very close to Kuala Lumpur and therefore is visited by large numbers of people at weekends (with attendant litter problems). However most people make for the swimming pool and stream in the eastern part of the park and trails beyond are fairly quiet. Here the secondary forest is an excellent place to see many of the lowland forest birds. On the western side Kancing Forest Recreation Reserve contains a popular waterfall. North of Templer Park, just outside it, is the clearly visible limestone outcrop of Bukit Takun which can be climbed in a few hours, although one section does require a bit of rock climbing. Inside the park, Bukit Anak (child of) Takun has an extensive cave network.

All these areas can be reached by either driving along the main Kuala Lumpur–Ipoh trunk road or by taking the Rawang bus from Pudu Raya bus stand and getting off at the 12 mile (20 kilometre) point for the eastern end of the park or the 14 mile (22 kilometre) point for the western end.

Taman Negara: Taman Negara, the National Park, is one of the best areas of primary tropical rainforest to visit. It is remote but at the headquarters there are chalets, a hostel and a campsite as well as a restaurant, so a stay can be very relaxing and comfortable.

Before going, it is necessary to book — well in advance during the April and August school holidays — and it is obligatory to get a permit. Contact the Department of Wildlife and National Parks, Block K 20, Government Offices Complex, Jalan Duta, Kuala Lumpur, (tel: 03-941272/941466). We found that attempts to make enquiries or to book by letter were futile unless we sent M$50 (US$20) deposit and M$1 (US$.50) for each permit. (This may have gone up.) Visitors from abroad do manage to get there, however, so the Department may be more sympathetic to overseas enquiries. Bear in mind that the park is closed from mid-November to mid-January and again during the Hari Raya (Malay New Year) holidays. Incidentally, it is a good idea to obtain, if it is in stock, the excellent trail guide when you make your bookings.

To reach Taman Negara you can drive to Jerantut via Temerloh on the Kuala Lumpur–Kuantan road or via Raub beyond Fraser's Hill. There are also buses and shared taxis to Jerantut. From here take the road (or a taxi) for 16 miles (26 kilometres) to Kuala Tembeling where there is a place to leave your car. Alternatively you can arrange for the train to Kota Bharu to stop at Tembeling Halt and hike through the plantations to the river bank. Boats to the park depart at 2 p.m. every day. Your bookings and permits will be checked and a place assigned in one of the boats. The journey to the headquarters up the Sungai Tembeling takes three hours.

It is possible to use the headquarters as a base for daily expeditions. You can also stay overnight at the various hides where there are bunk beds with rather mouldy mattresses and pillows. Book them at HQ and bring bedding, food and mosquito coils. Tabing Hide is only one hour's walk away. Kumbang Hide is five hours away on foot but can be reached by taking a boat for about 30 minutes up the Sungai Tembeling to Kuala Trenggan and then walking for an hour. The fishing lodge at Lata Berkoh, accessible either on foot or by boat on the Sungai Tahan has a lovely swimming hole and a reputation for fishing. Enormous fish can be caught (permits and equipment from HQ) but you generally need to go quite far up the river and have a helpful boatman to show you the best spots. (He'll probably catch the fish for you as well!)

Despite being in the heart of the forest in the centre of the peninsula, it may appear to you that there are relatively few animals. Sambar deer, wild pigs, squirrels and tree shrews are likely to be the complete list of mammals seen, especially as many animals are nocturnal. Gibbons call from Bukit Teresek in the mornings and seladangs (wild cattle) appear occasionally quite near HQ but the excitement of the forest is in imagining what you might see or what might be hiding. Sightings of tigers, elephants, panthers, tapirs and rhinos are always possibilities, however remote.

The plant and bird life will not disappoint. It would be pointless to attempt a complete bird list as our count ran to well over a hundred and many people have seen far more than us. February is an excellent time for bird-watching as the trees are usually fruiting then. We discovered one particular fig tree, just behind the office, laden with hornbills, fairy blue-birds (a magical blue) and several species of barbets, leafbirds and bulbuls. One bird to look out for is the two-foot-high crested fireback pheasant with its amazing blue facial skin. Its call resembles an angry squirrel. There are also many species of hornbills – listen for the maniacal laughter of the helmeted and goose-like quacking and steam train wingbeats of the rhinoceros hornbill. Drongos are the noisy, black long-tailed birds and the black and red broadbill, with its peculiar two-tone yellow and blue bill, is fairly common. And ... no – just set out with binoculars and your bird book and experience all the thrills yourself.

You can also venture further afield with camping equipment and guides from the headquarters. (Book in Kuala Lumpur and with luck the equipment will be available when you get there – liaison between Kuala Lumpur and HQ, however, can break down.) A favourite goal is Gunung Tahan which at 7,174 feet (2,187 metres) is the highest peak in the peninsula and is normally a nine-day round trip from the headquarters with an Orang Asli guide. It is a strenuous expedition and not really ideal for serious bird- or animal-watching as set campsites must be reached each evening and the pace is consequently quite fast.

It is possible to travel by boat further up the Sungai Tembeling past Kuala Trenggan to Kuala Kenyam, where there is a lodge, and from there either by boat or on foot (two hours) up the Sungai Kenyam to Kuala Perkai, where there is another lodge. Beyond this point there are no facilities for visitors but it is possible to proceed further by boat up the Sungai Tembeling to the Sungai Sat and Sungai Spia. The further upstream you go the clearer the water becomes and the more promising the fishing. When on treks, away from the HQ area, it is necessary to hire guides.

We met an American who had travelled right down the Tembeling and Pahang rivers to the coast on a raft, the whole journey taking almost ten days. He said that inland it was an exciting experience but that as he came nearer to the coast the trip became boring and extremely slow.

Pasoh: Pasoh Forest Reserve in Negri Sembilan state is a relatively undisturbed patch of lowland forest surrounded by oil palm monoculture. It is the site of a Forest Research Centre and has well established nature trails and a wonderful 115-foot (35-metre)-tall observation tree tower which affords an excellent view of the surrounding forest canopy at all levels. Accommodation in the hostel is cheap and bedding and cooking facilities are provided but food must be brought in. Permission to visit Pasoh can be got and bookings made from the Forest Research Institute, Kepong, Selangor.

To reach Pasoh, follow the road from Kuala Pilah in Negri Sembilan to Simpang Pertang. Just before this town turn right opposite the petrol station where the sign says FELDA Pasoh scheme. Thereafter follow the yellow arrows through the oil palm plantations for about two miles (three kilometres) to the Research Centre. Those without cars could get a bus or a collective taxi to Simpang Pertang and walk to the Forest Reserve.

Either way it is a place not to be missed by enthusiastic naturalists. Bird and plant life is extremely varied and among the more unusual animals to be found are white-handed gibbons, mouse deer and the slow loris. The last two may be spotted with luck by torchlight on a nocturnal walk in the forest.

Gunung Angsi and Gunung Telapak Burok: These are two interesting Mountain Forest Reserves in Negri Sembilan. Gunung Angsi (2,707 feet, 826 metres) although smaller, is a more strenuous climb, the last third being especially steep. The ascent takes about three to four hours. Bring food and water and it is advisable to wear long sleeves and long trousers as the path is overgrown in places. The view at the summit overlooks the whole Seremban valley. The entry track is on the left side of the Kuala Pilah-Seremban road, 13 miles (21 kilometres) from Kuala Pilah, at the beginning of a large uphill bend where there is a small stream. Follow the most obvious path for about half an hour until you come to a large open space. Cross, climb up a small bank and follow a steep track marked with red paint all the way to the summit.

Gunung Telapak Burok (3,917 feet, 1,195 metres), on the other hand, is reached by a winding road right to the summit where a relay station is located. There are scenic views of hill forests on both sides of the road. The terrain is rugged with plenty of palms and ferns. To get there, follow the road from Seremban to Kuala Klawang for about 14 miles (22 kilometres) until you reach the top of the Bukit Tangga pass which marks the boundary line between the Seremban and Jelebu districts. Turn right into a narrow road which leads up to the relay station. To be on the safe side, permission to enter both forest reserves can be obtained from the Seremban Forest Department, Seremban.

Sungai Endau/Endau–Rompin: The area of the upper Sungai Endau in the state of Johore is the last extensive wilderness area in the south of the peninsula. It has been explored little, is without mapped trails and is far from access by any road. This area, known as Endau–Rompin, has been proposed as a national park since the Third Malaysia Plan in the late seventies but forest policy is a state prerogative and Johore and Pahang, the two states concerned, have been very slow in gazetting the region. For any exploration written permission must be obtained from the Wildlife Department in Segamat (Johore). (This address is usually sufficient but for any additional queries contact the Department of Wildlife and National Parks in Kuala Lumpur.)

The most exciting way up the Sungai Endau is by canoe (your own) upstream from the river mouth just north of Mersing. The source of the river is to the east of Gunung Besar and the whole area, which is rich in wildlife, is particularly noted as being one of the last refuges of the tapir and the Sumatran rhinoceros. Plenty of jungle experience is essential for the Endau river trip. Travel light and be prepared to portage the canoe over shallow sections of water and major rapids.

The alternative way of getting to Endau–Rompin is by taking the Kluang–Mersing road as far as the Kahang police station and then turning north for more than an hour along laterite roads through oil palm plantations and several unsignposted junctions. Follow the telephone wires until you reach a fork just before an oil palm mill on the right. Keep left there and go past the Wildlife Department's checkpoint (show your papers) and on up the valley until the Sungai Endau can be seen on your right at a flood monitoring station. The road ahead soon becomes impassable except to four-wheel drive cars. Downstream from here is Kampong Peta, a small Orang Asli settlement; upstream is the proposed national park area.

There is a campsite with a deep, quiet pool for swimming to the east of Gunung Janing and west of the Sungai Endau, approximately 38 miles (61 kilometres) from the main road. In all it takes about three hours to get there from Kahang. This route can be followed through to the Pahang side of the proposed Endau–Rompin National Park but advice on this should be sought from the Department of Wildlife in Kuala Lumpur.

Gunung Besar: On the western edge of the proposed national park sits Gunung Besar (3,398 feet, 1,036 metres). It is visible to the east of the main trunk road north of Labis. It is possible to climb the mountain on a one-and-a-half to two-day trip but it is necessary to obtain a permit from the Department of Wildlife in Segamat. They can also provide a map and directions.

Ulu Lepar: This is an area of flat, lowland forest, well endowed with natural salt licks which attract a variety of herbivores. In addition, wildlife tends to concentrate here as surrounding areas are cleared for development. About one-fifth of the peninsula's estimated 500 seladangs are found here and for this reason the Department of Wildlife has set up a seladang unit on the banks of the Sungai Lepar. There are also numbers of elephants as well as tapirs, various species of deer and abundant bird life.

For a visit you may need permission from the Department of Wildlife and National Parks in Kuala Lumpur and it would be advisable to enquire about accommodation or camping possibilities. To reach the area you must leave the main Kuantan–Temerloh road at the village of Kampong Sri Jaya, about 35 miles (56 kilometres) west of Kuantan, and follow a laterite road which crosses the Sungai Lepar on a bridge beside the seladang unit's base camp. Wildlife is particularly abundant around two of the tributaries to the Sungai Lepar, the Sungai Berakit and the Sungai Rami. The former can be

reached by following the road for about three-quarters of a mile (one kilometre) beyond the bridge and then taking a timber track to the right for a
mile (one-and-a-half kilometres). The Sungai Rami flows into the Sungai
Lepar from the south about half a mile (one kilometre) upstream from the
bridge. There is a popular salt lick in this area.

THE HILL STATIONS

Most of the hill stations are primarily resort areas developed by the British
as retreats from the sweaty lowlands. Sunny days are like fresh European
ones and evenings can be chilly enough for woolly jumpers and wood fires.
Temperate flowers and vegetables flourish in this climate as do peculiar
primeval tree ferns. All the areas mentioned are well forested and while
animals are even less frequently seen than in the lowlands, a distinctive
range of bird life inhabits the higher altitudes.

The Cameron Highlands: This is the largest and best known of the hill
stations. It is a popular spot for Malaysian, Singaporean and foreign visitors
but it is more than a resort, having extensive tea plantations and vegetable
farms besides.

Tanah Rata, the main town of the Cameron Highlands district, is 37
miles (59 kilometres) from the town of Tapah on the main Kuala Lumpur—
Penang trunk road. The turn-off is well marked. Taxis and buses leave regularly from Tapah but be prepared for a very steep and winding climb.

Those with their own cars can take a little side trip before they begin
the ascent. Seven miles (11 kilometres) from Tapah a signpost marked Air
Panas (Hot Springs) directs you to the right and about half a mile (one
kilometre) from the turn-off, on the left, there is a parking area with chalets.
While the main body of the hot water is exhibited in a concrete tank some
still manages to trickle naturally into the side of the nearby river. This is a
fine place for a swim with forest trees hanging over the (shallow) water and
huge green and black Rajah Brooke butterflies flitting to and fro.

Incidentally, the road, if followed beyond the hot springs, continues for
several miles past Orang Asli settlements and through increasingly dense
forest to a dead end at a water pumping station.

There is a rest house in Tanah Rata (tel: 05-941254). It is a bit more
expensive than most and some find it a little gloomy but it has a lovely
situation and a wood fire (on request) in the evenings. There are plenty of
other hotels ranging from cheap, basic ones on Tanah Rata main street to
large plush and expensive ones. Beware — at holiday periods the whole place
tends to be booked solid so it's advisable to get in early.

The Cameron Highlands are well endowed with beautiful, quiet forest walks. A map giving details is available from the tourist office in Tanah Rata. Walk number five was one of our favourites. It begins at the MARDI Agricultural Research Station and goes through mossy forest with splendid epiphytic ferns on the trees. When it finally emerges by the golf course you can cut through side roads to link up with a short river walk (number four) coming out by the Garden Hotel, thus completing a circuit back to Tanah Rata.

The Robinson Falls walk, number eight, is popular owing to the love Malaysians have for waterfalls, but beyond this point you meet few other people. The trail can be followed right down into the valley to link with a side road to the Boh tea plantation. Once on the main road it is fairly easy to hitch back to Tanah Rata.

The Boh tea plantation is in fact worth a visit. Look out for the sign between Ringlet and Tanah Rata near what must be the biggest purple bougainvillaea bush in the country. The road narrows at the gates and curves up and through hillsides of toy-town-neat rows of tea bushes, dotted with pink flowers. At the top is a tea processing shed and if it is open you will be welcomed and shown around.

Gunung Brinchang (6,562 feet, 2,000 metres) is the highest peak. You can reach it by car but the road is extremely steep. There are good views to be had at the top. However, as clouds tend to gather here it's best to arrive early in the morning. You can also walk up and down — a very rewarding trip which takes the best part of a day.

Of the many birds to be seen in the Cameron Highlands perhaps the loveliest are the silver-eared mesias — bright yellow, red, black and grey birds with white cheeks which gather in noisy parties. The most vivid bird you see will undoubtedly be the mountain (grey-chinned) minivet. The male is bright fluorescent red and the female yellow, both with black backs and wings. Barbets are solitary heavy green birds with colourful heads; the golden-throated and the fire-tufted frequent the highlands, the latter distinctive for its loud cicada-like buzzing call. Leafbirds are well named for their pure green plumage but the mountain one, the orange-bellied leafbird has, as its name suggests, a beautiful orange belly and a black and blue chin. Even the most sedentary visitor to the hill stations is likely to get a good look at the black-throated sunbird as it feeds on the flowering bushes and lets you come within a couple of feet of it. Its head and throat are a glossy metallic purplish blue, its back maroon and belly yellow.

Before you leave the Cameron Highlands don't forget to visit the market beyond Brinchang or, even better, Mr Subramaniam at Green Farm a little further up and stock up with produce — oranges, tomatoes, leeks, cauliflowers, beetroot . . . the list of temperate climate delights is endless.

Genting Highlands: This resort is about an hour's drive from Kuala Lumpur. It is also accessible by bus from Pahang Bus Stand, Jalan Pekililing, taxi or helicopter. It is best known for its casino and de luxe hotels. There are no trails like those in the Cameron Highlands but there are plenty of forested slopes to clamber around on. Look out for pitcher plants which trap and digest insects in their pitcher-shaped modified leaves.

Fraser's Hill: This is a small, peaceful little resort about two hours' drive from Kuala Lumpur. On the main road north from Kuala Lumpur turn inland at Kuala Kubu Baru and continue to The Gap. From there the final five miles (eight kilometres) is on a one-way road, traffic going up on the odd hours (for 40 minutes) and down on even hours. If travelling by bus change at Kuala Kubu Baru.

Accommodation at Fraser's Hill itself is quite expensive and although there is a rest house it is often full at weekends. We always stayed at The Gap rest house, bookable, as in the case of the Fraser's Hill one, through the government office in Kuala Kubu Baru (tel: 03-341026/7). This large rest house has a magnificent setting, perched opposite dense forest which is alive with bands of leaf monkeys and bird life. The evenings are an ideal temperature. Have tea or a beer on the verandah and grapple with the logic of the eccentric waiter. Spectacular numbers of moths and insects are attracted to the lights after dark.

Most of the few forest paths in Fraser's Hill are overgrown and impassable but there are lots of quiet roads, in particular up the hill past the Merlin Hotel. Bird life is similar to that of the Cameron Highlands but even more abundant because little of Fraser's Hill has been cultivated. Particularly noticeable are large niltivas – quiet, dark flycatchers with (males) bright blue heads and neck patches – and the noisy, heavy, chestnut-capped laughing thrushes. The buzzing of fire-tufted barbets is a constant background noise.

Maxwell Hill: This is one of the oldest and least developed of the hill stations rising to 3,400 feet (1,037 metres) above the town of Taiping in Perak. Access up the steep, winding seven-mile (11 kilometre) road is by government Land Rover only, unless you want to walk. The Land Rovers leave on the hour from the far end of the Lake Gardens. Places are limited and can be booked in advance – definitely advisable at weekends and holidays. There is a rest house at the top (tel: 05-886241) and there are quiet roads for walks.

Penang Hill: This is a popular spot (2,700 feet, 823 metres), easily reached by funicular railway. It is also possible to walk up, starting at the Moon Gate in the Botanical Gardens. Penang Hill Hotel, with 12 rooms, is well run and a young Indian called Shanmuggarn is on call to guide visitors on the hill trails. He is not a biologist but was born on the hill, knows the trails well and is knowledgeable about the use of plants in herbal medicine.

Further Reading

Politics and Islam

Mahathir bin Mohamad, *The Malay Dilemma*, Federal Publications, Singapore, 1977 (3rd reprint). (Interesting for the Malaysian Prime Minister's outspoken views on race of 15 years ago.)

Comber, Leon, *13 May 1969: A Historical Survey of Sino-Malay Relations*, Heinemann Educational Books (Asia) Limited, 1983. (An extremely readable and short background explanation of the causes of the 1969 racial riots.)

Hua Wu Yin, *Class and Communalism in Malaysia: Politics in a Dependent Capitalist State*, Zed Books Limited in conjunction with Marram Books, 1983. (A socialist view of Malaysia's problems.)

Miller, Harry, *Jungle War in Malaya: The Campaign against Communism 1948–60*, Arthur Barker, 1972, Eastern Universities Press, 1981. (An informative if one-sided view of events during the Malayan Emergency.)

Naipaul, V. S., *Among the Believers – An Islamic Journey*, Andre Deutsch, 1981. Reprinted in Penguin. (Excellent book on Islam with a chapter on Malaysia.)

History

Bird, Isabella L., *The Golden Chersonese: Travels in Malaya in 1879*, John Murray, 1883. Oxford in Asia Paperbacks, 1980. (Probably the most entertaining of the early writings on Malaya.)

Innes, Emily, *The Chersonese with the Gilding Off*, Oxford in Asia Historical Reprints, 1974. (Originally published in 1885, this book, seen from the perspective of the wife of a junior British official, presents a far less glamorous picture of the Malay Peninsula than Isabella Bird's writings – nonetheless, it makes fascinating reading.)

Nature

King, Ben, Woodcock, Martin and Dickinson, E. C., *Field Guide to the Birds of S. E. Asia*, William Collins, Sons and Company Limited, Glasgow, 1975. (Indispensable for bird enthusiasts.)

MALAYSIAN NATURE HANDBOOKS:

Tweedie, M. W. F., *Mammals of Malaysia*, Longman Malaysia, 1978.

Tweedie, M. W. F., *Common Birds of the Malay Peninsula*, Longman Malaysia, 1979.

(Other excellent books in this series are *Common Malayan Butterflies*,

Common Malayan Wildflowers, Common Malaysian Fruits and *Coral Reefs of Malaysia.*)

Maxwell, Sir George, *In Malay Forests*, Blackwood & Sons, Ltd, 1907. Eastern Universities Press, Singapore, 1982. (A collection of fine descriptive writings in spite of some purple prose excesses.)

Shuttleworth, Charles, *Malaysia's Green and Timeless World: An Account of the Flora, Fauna and Indigenous Peoples of the Forests of Malaysia*, Heinemann Educational Books (Asia) Limited, 1981. (The best general book on Malaysia's wildlife.)

Fiction

Burgess, Anthony, *The Long Day Wanes: A Malayan Trilogy*, Heinemann 1956, 1958, 1959. Reprinted by Penguin. (The trilogy is an extremely amusing novel about life in crumbling, colonial Malaya.)

Fauconnier, Henri, *Malaisie*, (Paris, Stock, 1930) *The Soul of Malaya.* (Trans. Eric Sutton) Oxford in Asia. Reprinted 1980. (Considered by many to be the best novel written about Malaya.)

Maugham, W. Somerset, *Collected Short Stories*, Heinemann, 1951. Reprinted by Pan. (Volumes 2 and particularly 4 have short stories about Malaya.)

Theroux, Paul, *The Consul's File*, Hamish Hamilton, 1977. Reprinted by Penguin. (Amusing and apocryphal short stories.)

Guides

Insight Guides, *Malaysia*, Apa Productions Limited. Ninth Edition, 1984. (Beautiful photographs.)

Holmes, Genevieve, *Malaysia: A Guide to the Peninsula*, Roger Lascelles, 1983. (Useful for travel details.)

Loose, Stefan and Ramb, Renate, *Malaysia Handbook*, Stefan Loose, 1985. (An English translation of the most popular German guide to the area, packed with practical information.)

Wheeler, Tony, *Malaysia, Singapore and Brunei: A Travel Survival Kit*, Lonely Planet, 1982. (Has supplanted the original traveller's bible *South East Asia on a Shoestring* in these countries.)

STELLA MARTIN was born in Northern Ireland. She has lived and worked in Amsterdam, Tokyo and Malaysia.

DENIS WALLS was born in Kilmarnock, Scotland and has taught English in Algeria and France as well as in Malaysia.

Since writing this book Stella and Denis have moved from the East to the East End (of London) where they are appalled to find themselves paying the equivalent of 240 durians in monthly rent. Denis now works at an international school and Stella writes magazines for young English learners.